Otters
Return to the River

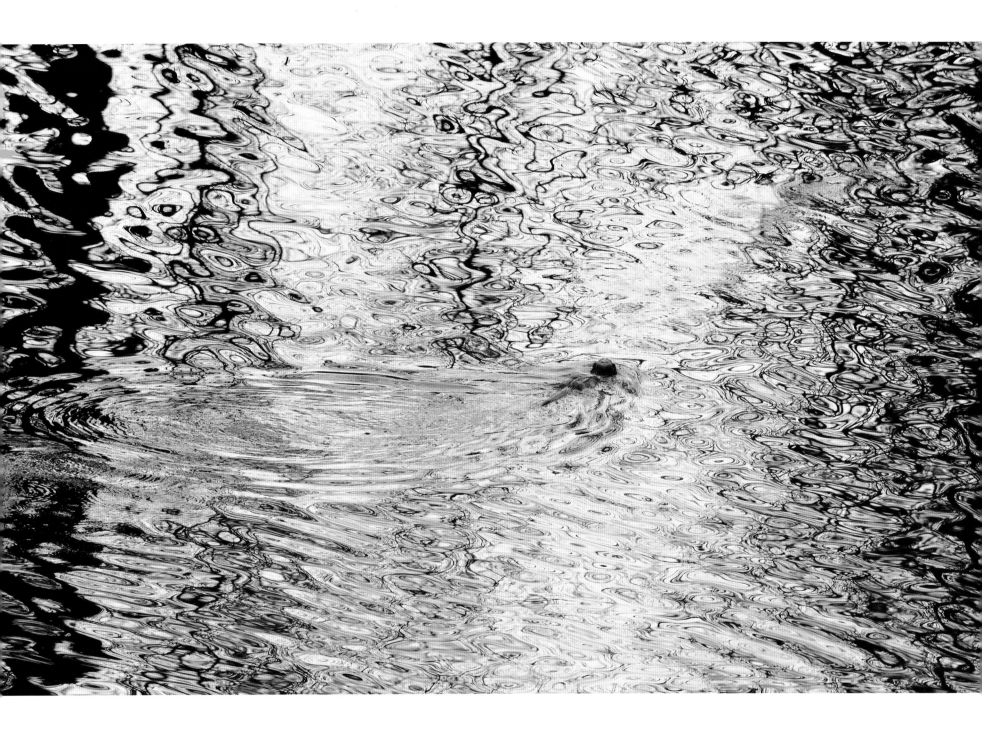

Otters
Return to the River

Laurie Campbell and Anna Levin

BIRLINN

To my Grandfather,
Colin Chisam

With thanks to Derek Robeson
and Roger Manning

L.C

For Rob Meijer,
with love and thanks

A.L

First published in 2014 by
Birlinn Limited
West Newington House
10 Newington Road
Edinburgh
EH9 1QS
www.birlinn.co.uk

ISBN: 978 1 78027 206 1

British Library Cataloguing-in-Publication Data
A catalogue record for this book is available from
the British Library

Designed and typeset by Mark Blackadder

Printed and bound by Hussar Books, Poland

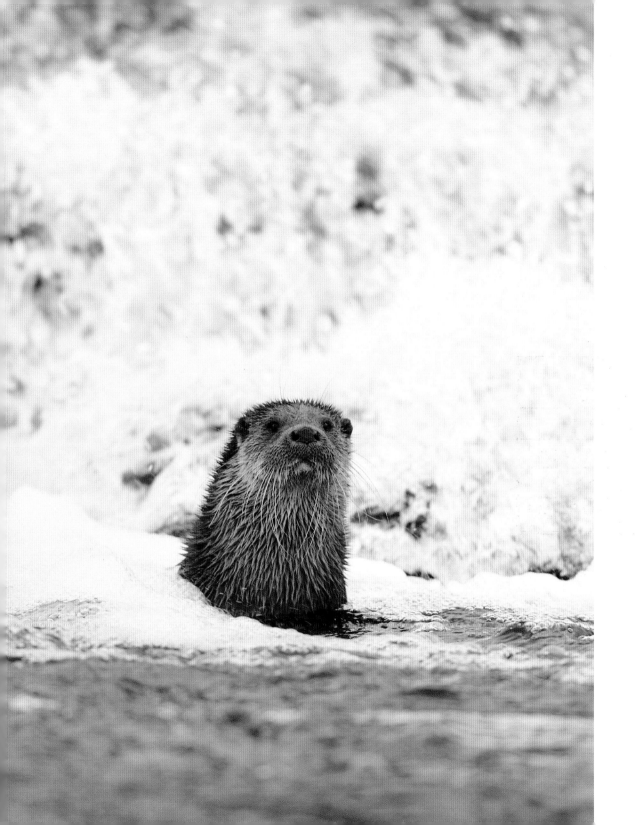

Contents

Foreword

It was the late Eileen Soper, the celebrated 1960s wildlife artist whose delicate sketches gave her books such enduring charm, who famously wrote: 'Badger watchers are not entirely human.' She was right, as much of herself as of other naturalists who have striven to become one with their wild subjects. She might just as well have been speaking of Laurie Campbell. It was Laurie's wife, Margaret, who told me that she couldn't remember when Laurie was last on time for supper. I don't think she was joking.

In admiration of dazzling wildlife photography people often say to me, 'Oh, he must have such patience!' And, yes, patience is an important ingredient, but imagining that all you have to do is sit still and the rest will fall into place, grossly underrates the reality. You could sit on a riverbank for the rest of your life and never see an otter unless you also knew what you were doing, far less take a sequence of photographs to match the exquisite work of the immensely skilled perfectionist in these pages. And there I go again – it isn't just perfectionism or technical skill or patience or knowledge or enthusiasm or experience – although, of course, to some degree all of those are important. You could possess any combination of those faculties and still fail dismally to produce images like Laurie's. No, it's what Eileen Soper was referring to: that exceptional ability to slough off human-ness and blend seamlessly and invisibly into the wild world – to become a part of it – so that it accepts you and opens up to you.

I'm a point-and-press man. My photographic achievements equate to the holiday efforts of an impetuous twelve year old. But I am a field naturalist who has spent many thousands of hours trying to be 'at one' with wildlife. So I think I understand Laurie's technique, his route into the private world of the otter, or the badger, the kingfisher or the roe deer – even the wild wood or the river itself.

In Anna Levin's luminous text the word 'intuitive' and the sense of Laurie being guided by an unspoken intuition crops up over and over again; and rightly so. Laurie's approach is perhaps as much as or more than 50 per cent intuition: a sixth sense that has been honed to razor keenness by the hours, days, months, years – now decades – he has spent out there, alone, shedding his human self, watching, listening, learning, just being there. Wordsworth expressed it brilliantly: *'I have felt a presence that disturbs me with the joy of elevated thoughts...'* It's a sense that rings in Laurie's head when he knows that something is right: a place, a time, a moment, a presence... and, sure enough, there is the otter. That's when all the rest kick into play: the technical skill, the patience, the years of experience, the hunkering down as still as a rock

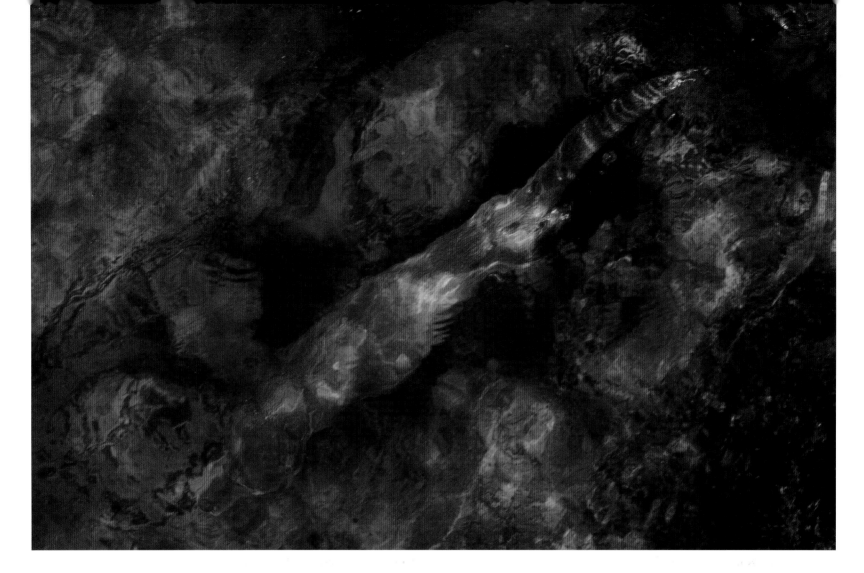

for hours on end, the perfectionism. But the intuition has to come first.

I have known Laurie for many years; every summer he stays with us in the Highlands, although I would never presume to join him on his secretive forays into the wild. I know very well what it is to work with nature, work that must be done alone. That is why I think it was so courageous of them both to have Anna Levin tagging along with her eagle eye and her notebook. But I am very glad that they pulled it off. In clean, unfussy prose as crisp as the photographs, Anna has caught the master at his trade and the rippling River Tweed and its lissom otters, and blended them together in these pages so that we can all be out there, with the dew forming on Laurie's long vigils, silent as snow, watching, watching . . .

How splendid that the otter has returned to the Tweed, but I'm afraid there's no sign of improvement; Laurie is still always late for supper.

John Lister-Kaye
House of Aigas, March 2014

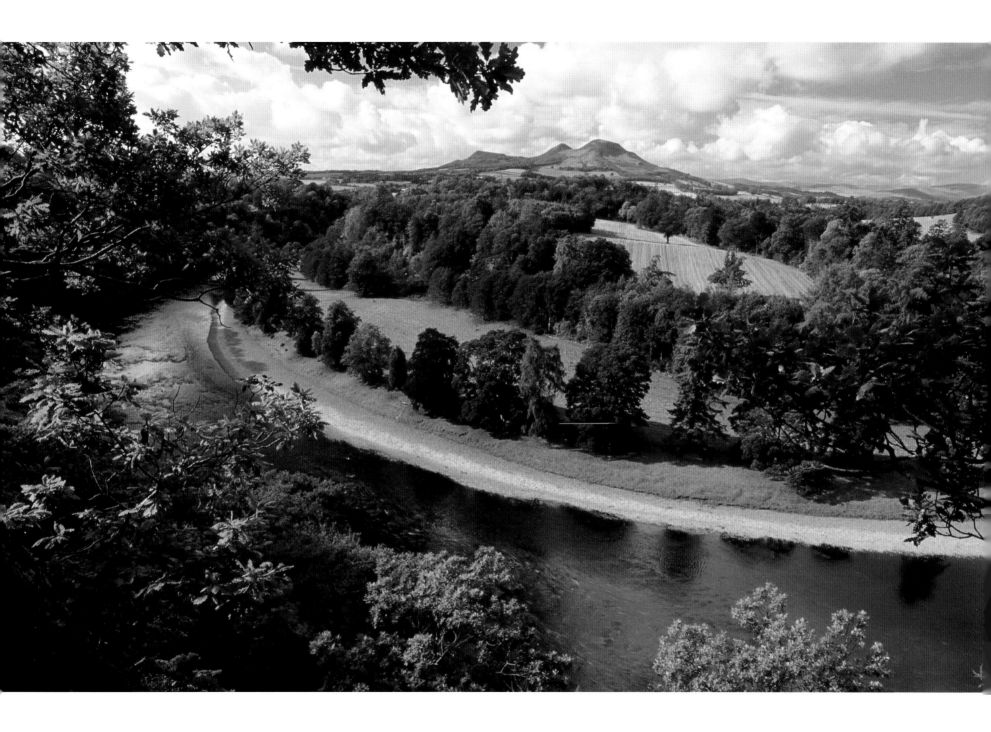

Introduction

This is a story about a man, a wild animal and a river. Their narratives overlap and intertwine, looping around each other like otters at play. They're part of a bigger picture – as all stories are – tugged by tides and swept up in wider currents, and, in turn, their stories reach others far beyond their own, their ripples flowing outwards in concentric circles.

The river is the Tweed, including its many tributaries, which pour down from the surrounding hills and swell the main artery throughout its 100-mile-long journey to the North Sea. It is world renowned for its salmon: records from the Bronze Age suggest that as long as people have lived beside the Tweed they've been fishing there.

The Tweed rises from Silurian bedrock high in the Southern Uplands and gathers strength as it tumbles down from the moors towards the fertile plain below, rolling over red sandstone and winding its way eastwards, curving under bridges and through the Borders towns, forming the long-contested border between Scotland and England for most of its last twenty miles. In its lower reaches it settles and broadens over limestone, then slows and spreads, salty now, into the estuary at Berwick-upon-Tweed.

The animal is the Eurasian otter *Lutra lutra*, the only wild otter in the British Isles. As reflected in its name, its geographical range stretches throughout Europe and Asia, from Ireland to eastern Russia, and extends to the tip of North Africa, thereby occupying the largest area of any otter species. *Lutra lutra* is part of a worldwide family of otters with thirteen species, including the two-metre-long giant otters of the Amazon and the sea otters of the Californian coastline, as well as more obscure species, such as the hairy-nosed and Congo clawless otter. All

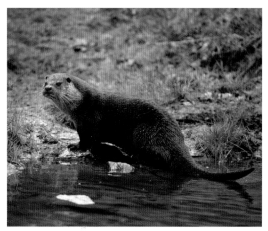

Above. A captive otter in a wildlife park. At one time most available images of otters were taken in captive situations.

Opposite. Looking over the Tweed from a popular view-point known as Scott's View, into the patchwork river valley.

otters are members of the weasel family of carnivores, the Mustelidae, as are badgers, polecats, martens, stoats and mink. Otters share

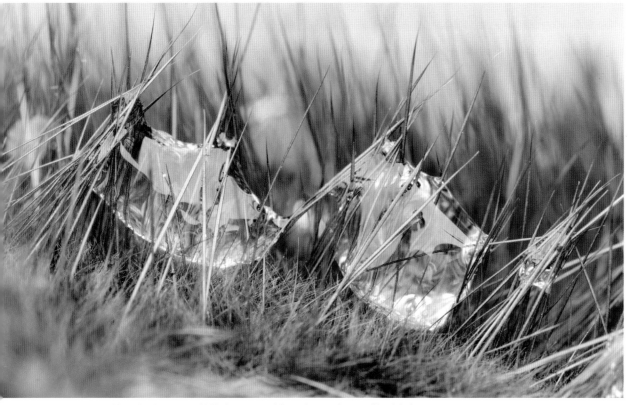

Looking closely at a road-killed otter, I could see the two layers of its rich fur coat: long guard hairs hold the drops of water away from the soft, warm underfur.

some physical traits with their mustelid relations, such as long bodies, short legs, strong jaws and sharp teeth.

Once upon a time *Lutra lutra* was widespread in the British Isles. Though elusive by nature, being mostly nocturnal and solitary, the otter was an integral part of the landscape at the water's edge, whether lake or wetland, river or sea. Their presence was neatly captured in Kenneth Grahame's 1908 novel *The Wind in the Willows*: while Ratty, Mole, Toad and Badger take centre stage on the riverbank, Otter appears and disappears, a strong yet mysterious character on the sidelines.

Otters have been hunted by man since ancient times, for their rich fur coats, for the protection of fish stocks and for sport. Hunting otters for sport was a popular activity in Britain in the nineteenth and twentieth centuries; otter-hounds were bred especially for this purpose, with local hunts organised throughout the country. In *Tarka the Otter*, published in 1927, Henry Williamson vividly describes the ever-present threat of the hunt in the life of a British otter.

The otter hunters were among the first to notice that otters were disappearing from Britain's waterways in the early 1960s. The hunts were out searching for signs of their presence in the places they had always been and it became evident that there were far fewer otters around. The hunts restricted their kills, but otter numbers continued to decline. And it wasn't just the otter that was disappearing; huge numbers of birds were dying, too, especially birds of prey, such as peregrine falcons and sparrowhawks.

The culprit was found to be toxic chemicals that had been introduced in the 1950s. Organochlorines such as aldrin and dieldrin were used as pesticides for sheep dips and seed dressings, among many other uses. Small songbirds were poisoned directly by feeding on dressed seed, and predators were poisoned by feeding on the seed-eaters. Many birds and animals also suffered the insidious effects from sub-lethal poisoning, where the presence of toxins affected their physiology, behaviour and reproduction.

Residues from the fields and sheep dip were washed into the rivers and watercourses and

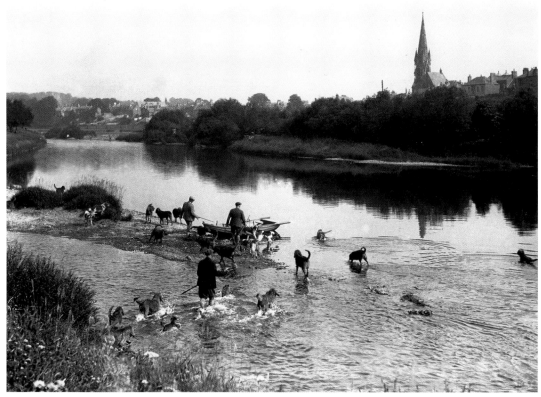

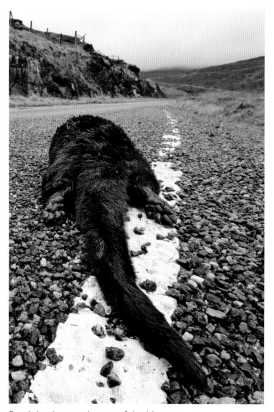

Otter hunting on the Tweed at Kelso's Junction Pool. Hunting with hounds continued into the 1970s – otters received legal protection in England and Wales in 1978 and then in Scotland in 1982.

Road deaths remain one of the biggest threats to otter populations today.

began to accumulate in the food chain, from microorganisms to small fish to large fish and on to fish-eating birds and mammals. As top predators, otters were receiving the greatest concentration of these toxins. This was augmented by widespread habitat destruction, increasing road deaths and decreasing fish stocks, and by the late 1970s otters had disappeared from most of Britain and much of Europe. However, small pockets remained in the west and north of England, and in Wales, while Scotland's islands and western seaboard remained a stronghold.

It took time for the effects of these poisons to be understood and the extent of the massacre to be acknowledged, for the legislative wheels to turn and for the use of these substances to be gradually banned. It took longer still for the levels of toxins to slowly reduce in the bodies of predators; however, over many generations the effects diminished, birds of prey reclaimed the skies and fish returned to the rivers.

Otters were slower to recover. But the loss of otters caused widespread concern and a raft of measures was put in place to save them from the threat of local extinction: waterways were cleaned up, special otter habitats were created

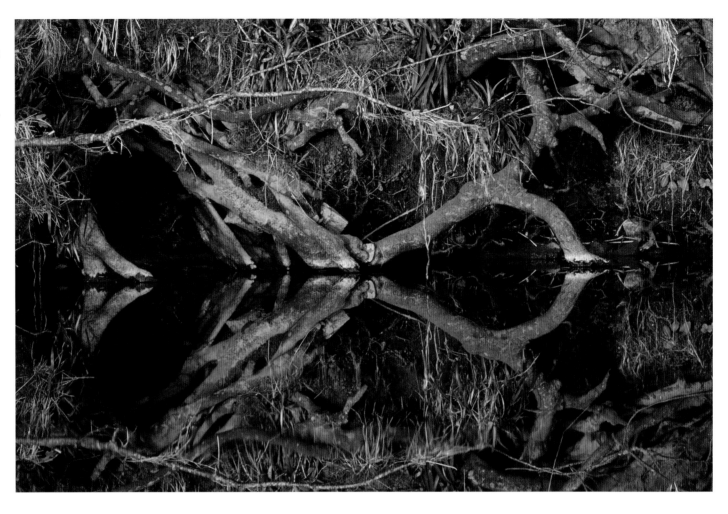

and both eel nets and crayfish traps were modified to prevent entanglement. There were attempts to address the problem of road deaths with tunnels, culverts and fencing to direct otters to safer routes. Otters were given increasing legal protection, first hunting was banned and later their place of shelter protected from disturbance. In some areas captive-bred otters were released into the wild in reintroduction programmes to assist their recovery.

Gradually – as the chemical load reduced, the water quality improved and fish supply increased – Britain's rivers became fit for otters again. And so otters spread through the country, sending ripples of excitement along the rivers. Although a cause of concern to some anglers and freshwater fisheries, the return of otters was greeted with delight by the general public. Otters had been largely unseen for a generation, yet the species had only gained in popularity, reaching something akin to celebrity status in the animal world. In a BBC *Wildlife* magazine poll in 2008, otters beat even badgers and dolphins to the top spot of Britain's

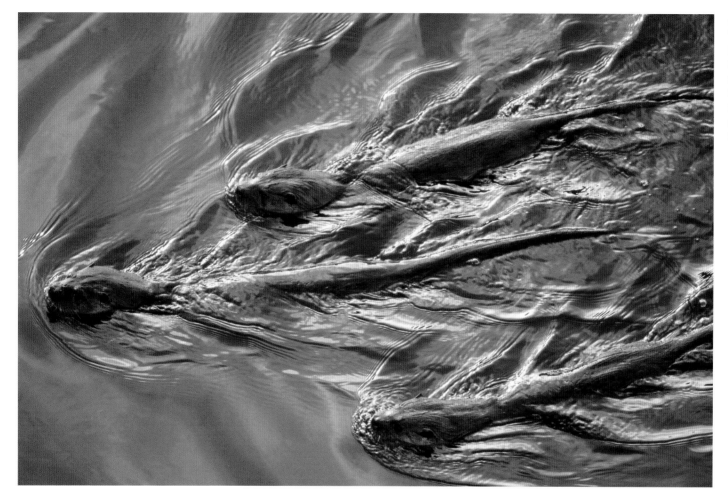

A mother with her two grown cubs, photographed in the middle of a Saturday afternoon from the seventeenth-century road bridge in the centre of Berwick-upon-Tweed.

favourite mammal. Though they share a hint of menace with their mustelid cousins, otters are much admired for their good looks and charm, and the utter grace and beauty of their movement in water. Stories, both fiction and non-fiction, have played a part in their popularity. Among others, Williamson's Tarka and Gavin Maxwell's Chuhala, Mijbil and Edal – described in *Ring of Bright Water* – have given otters a special place in the storyland of our hearts.

Otters continued to reclaim their place in the country's waterways, spreading eastwards from their former strongholds and settling into both rural and urban environments. A national survey in 2002 found otters had re-colonised just over a third of their former sites; a subse-quent survey ten years later found signs of otters at nearly two-thirds of these. In 2011, the Environment Agency made a jubilant announcement that otters had returned to every county in England, proclaiming Kent as the last piece in the jigsaw of otter recovery.

Yet some scientists warn that estimates of otter numbers may be exaggerated and contest

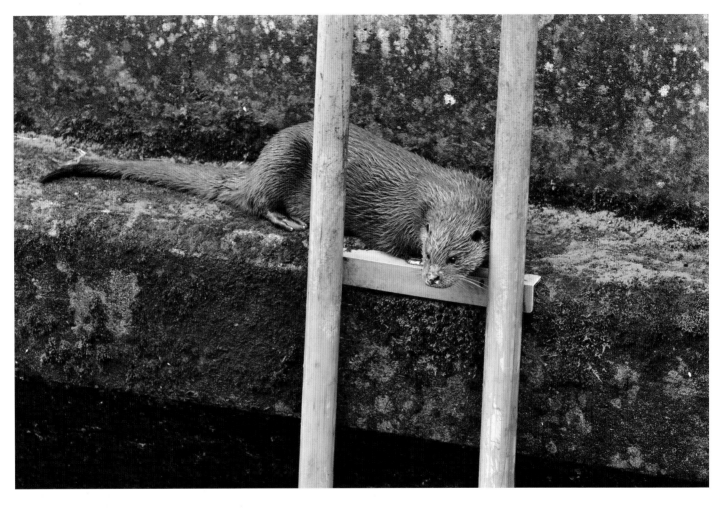

I spotted this otter in the middle of an autumn day on a hydro dam on the River Beauly. I presume otters were taking advantage of the fish moving and stacking up beneath the dam.

the survey methods used to calculate the population of this elusive animal. They fear that over-playing the otters' return could provoke a backlash, particularly from those managing valuable fish stocks, and that this could challenge the legal protection that otters have gained. Otter populations are still fragile, road deaths are high and post-mortems have revealed disturbing findings about their reproductive health, which have been linked to endocrine disrupting chemicals (EDCs) in the waterways. It may be that having recovered from one era of pollutants, otters now face the threat of another. So while there's no doubt that otters are back, continued vigilance is needed to ensure they remain so.

Meanwhile, the Tweed has fared even better than most rivers in the big clean-up of recent decades and is now one of the least polluted rivers in the UK. An unusual confluence of geography and local government has meant that most of the river catchment is under the management of one authority, enabling integrated planning of the land and water as a

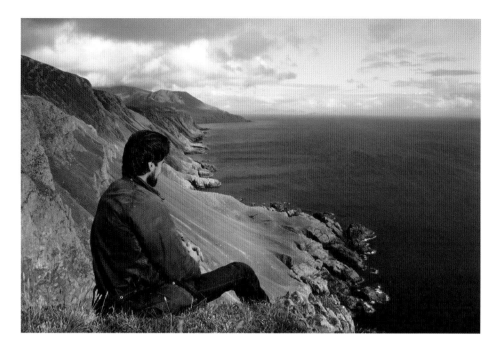

whole. A range of environmental organisations are also working in partnership with farmers and landowners to restore a more natural river system: opening up salmon routes; restoring natural curves in the tributaries; establishing woodlands, wetlands, hedges, meadows and ponds. Flood prevention work has led to a greater awareness that river management begins high in the hills. All this and more contributes to a river system better able to regulate itself, and to support wildlife.

And so into these bigger stories of geology, ecology, history and politics, steps the photographer Laurie Campbell. Born a stone's throw from the Tweed, he spent much of his childhood exploring the river and its wildlife. He's stayed closely connected to the Tweed all his life, travelling throughout Scotland but always returning to his home river. He became well acquainted with *Lutra lutra* when his work took him to the then strongholds of Scotland's western shores. When otters found their way back to the rich waters of the Tweed and its tributaries, Laurie was there, ready and waiting – senses finely tuned and camera poised – to tell their story.

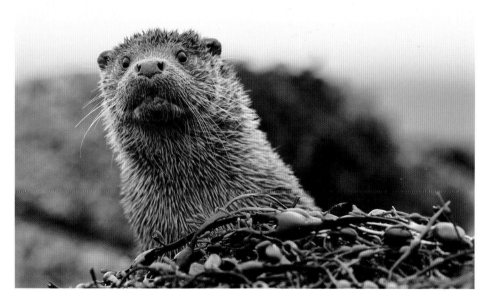

Top. Looking out over the cliffs of Rum, in the mid-1980s, while photographing feral goats for the American Museum of Natural History.

Left. On the shores of North Harris, I was lying low under camouflage netting – not recognizable as a human to this curious otter, which came out of the sea to find out what I was.

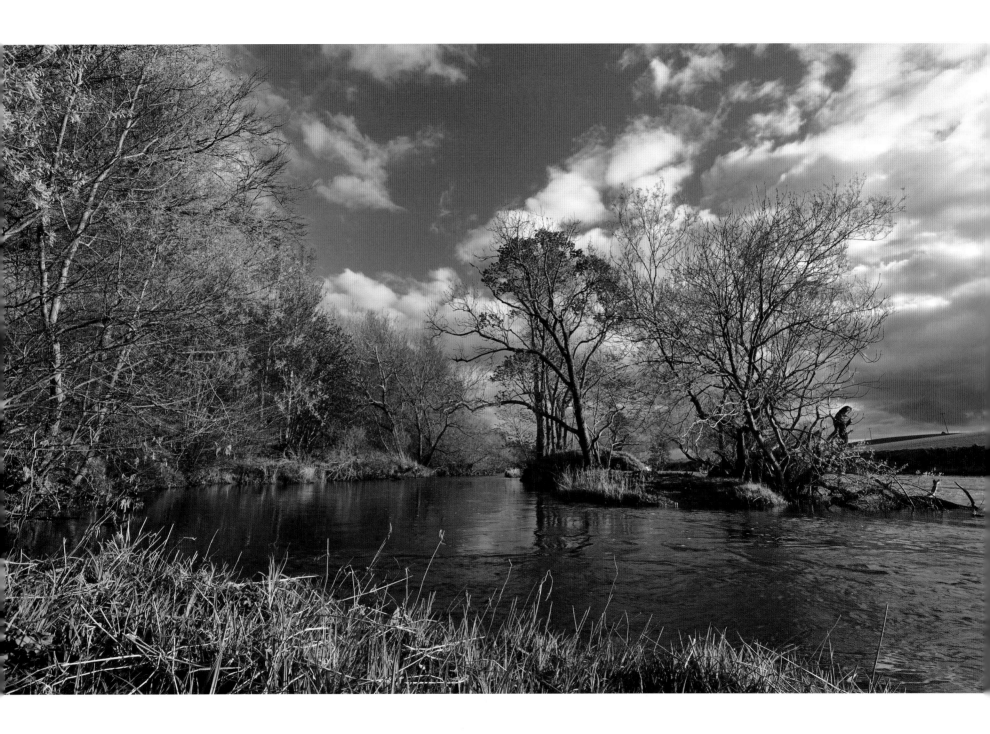

Chapter 1 Spring

Spring summons a rush of new life, bringing sounds, colours and vibrant activity to the river. As the days get longer and lighter, plant life takes off as if a race is starting, and the riverbanks are bright with the fresh greens of new growth.

There is new life among the otter families too, with young cubs out and about, sticking close to their mothers as they learn to master their watery environment. As well as a wide range of fish species, the otters are feeding on seasonal windfalls such as frogs, common toads, birds' eggs and ducklings.

It's a time of plenty for a nature photographer as well – a wealth of light and time after the short days of winter, and much to keep me occupied as I watch and wait for otters. I see oystercatchers hanging around in pairs – they moved inland from the coast weeks ago to stake their claim on favoured breeding territories. The male mallards are noisy, squabbling and fighting over mates, then by late April there are noticeably fewer female mallards on the river, as by then they're sitting on eggs. Willow catkins by the water attract the first bumblebees and their humming buzz is a backdrop to spring days on the river, along with the sweet, melodious songs of summer migrants such as willow warblers and sedge warblers.

I set off to look for otters on this bright evening in April, it was about 7 p.m. and the sky was so blue and the air had that startling freshness about it – a clean, clear atmosphere after a day of rain clouds and showers. Spring is a lovely time for photographing otters because the bankside vegetation is coming through and the trees are coming into leaf – all creating a lively backdrop of shiny, new, vivid green but not yet obscuring the view of the river. I could feel a tangible sense of optimism in the air and I wanted to capture that feeling of promise.

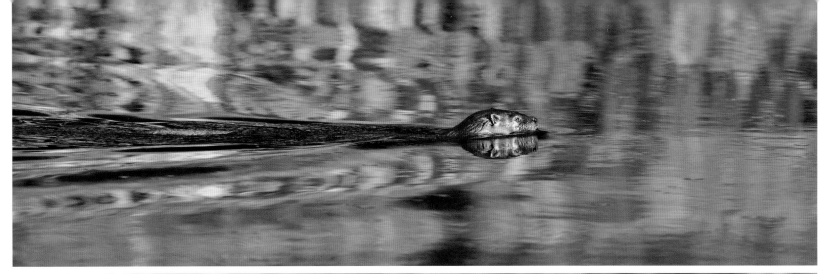

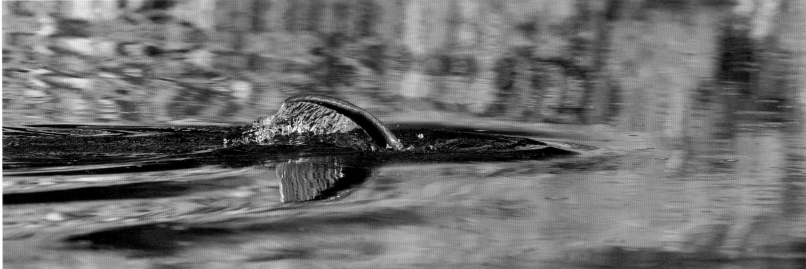

Spring sunshine lit these feel-good pictures, taken early in the fresh green of an early May morning. This otter is moving purposefully downstream in mid-river, heading back to its holt after spending a night out hunting.

I was able to photograph each stage of the characteristic 'Loch Ness monster' shape of an otter swimming: the head low on the water's surface, the hump of its back as it rolls and lastly a wave of the long, tapered tail.

Sometimes a single otter looks like three separate creatures, and when several are playing together, all looping and twisting around each other, all you see is rolling humps and tails and heads – it can be hard to tell what belongs to which!

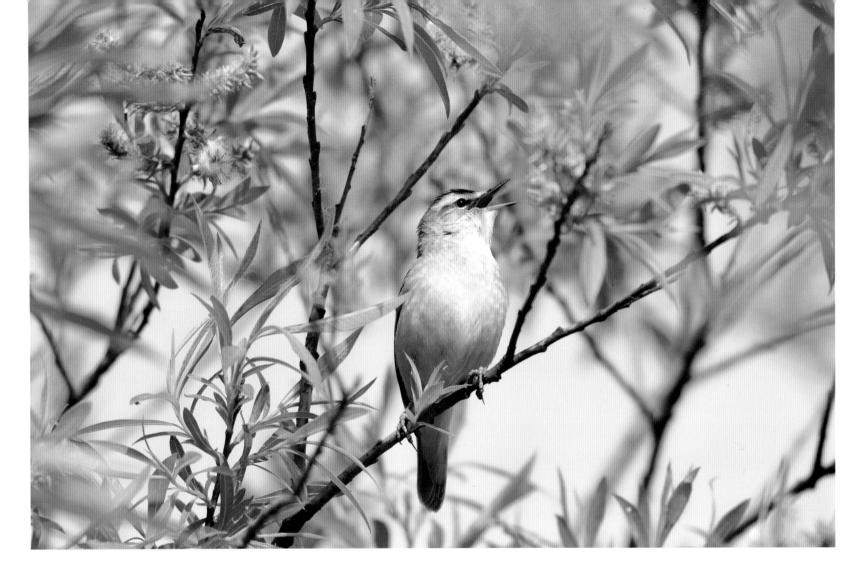

The songs of migrant warblers brighten the riverbank from early May. Warblers are often referred to by novice birders as 'little brown jobs' as they're quite difficult to distinguish from each other visually – willow warblers from chif-fchaffs for example. In the early days when I'd set out with my *Observer's Book of Birds*, the sedge warbler was the one I could identify quickly and reliably due to its whirring call and dark band across the eye. It has been instantly recognisable to me ever since. Sedge warblers show themselves clearly, proclaiming their territory from a prominent place, unlike some other warbler species that are more often heard but not seen.

I was on the riverbank photographing mute swans on a May morning when I heard this sedge warbler behind me. I took some pictures from a distance, then after a bit of stalking moved closer to refine my position and settle beneath a bit of camouflage netting. It retreated to thicker cover but returned to the same twig to continue its song.

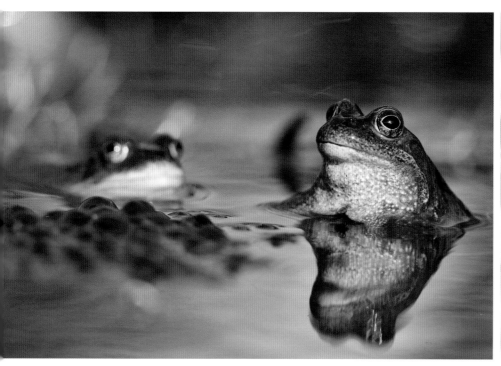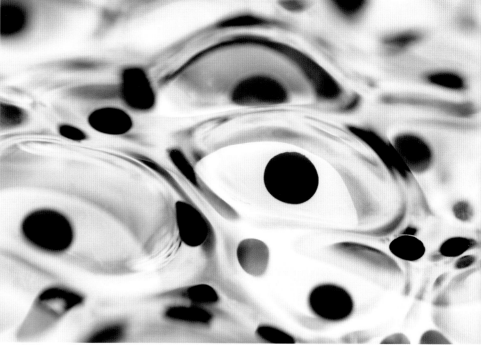

Gathering to spawn in springtime a few weeks before the common toads, common frogs also offer rich pickings for otters. Without the poisonous skin glands of common toads, frogs are a more palatable food source and so are taken by a wider range of predators, including foxes, grey herons and common buzzards.

Photographing close-ups of field signs can tell a story in a new way. I enjoy capturing a few square inches of nature and presenting them in a way that makes people hesitate, look more closely and seek to understand and appreciate.

For me, like many others, frogs are symbolic of spring. They bring back childhood memories of going out with jam jars to collect frogspawn and bringing it home to watch in rapt fascina-tion as the transformation takes place from blobs to wriggling tadpoles to tiny frogs.

Meanwhile, on the riverbanks, these tiny, thumbnail-sized beginnnings of Himalayan balsam show how efficiently this invasive plant covers the ground, barely giving other plants a chance. By midsummer, these can reach almost six feet in height, with clusters of deep pink

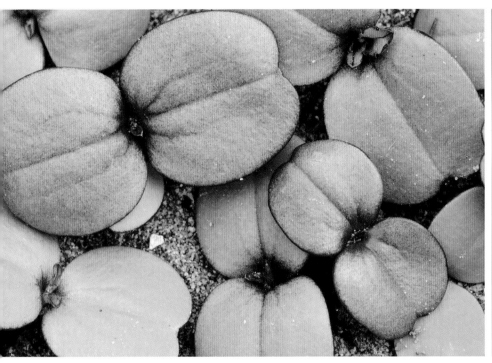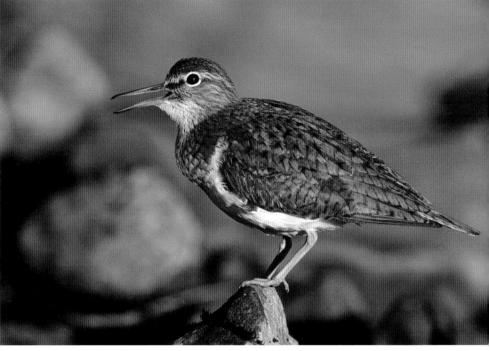

pendulous flowers.

Whenever I am close to freshwater, the high-pitched piping call of common sandpipers is equivalent to the arrival of the first cuckoo and epitomises the sound of spring.

I once visited the Scottish naturalist John Morton Boyd when he was working on his autobiographical book *The Song of the Sand-piper*. We shared stories about our experiences in the Highlands and he told me about his field trips from decades earlier, sleeping in the back of a Land Rover, whilst surveying tracts of land to establish which areas ought to become Scotland's very first National Nature Reserves.

One of the things that he mentioned was that sandpipers seemed omnipresent, not just in Scotland but in so many parts of the world as well. He was widely travelled and sandpipers gave him a feeling of connection, as he'd hear that familiar call wherever he went.

I only met him the once, but he was one of those people I wish I'd met a lot sooner. I often think about our meeting when I hear the sandpiper's song.

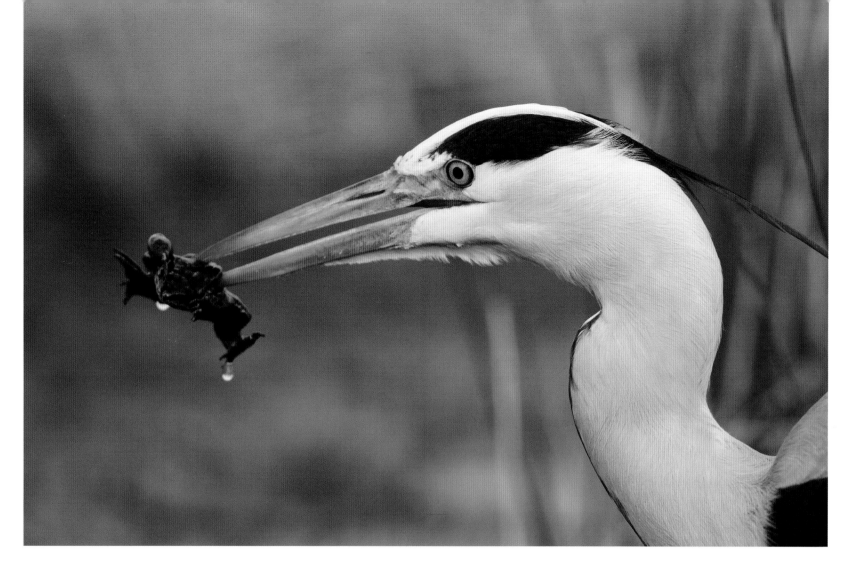

There's a farm pond surrounded by boggy ground close to our village where I have established a semi-permanent wooden hide. Here I can photograph common snipe from autumn to spring. Over the years I've noticed that such important wetlands have become increasingly rare, as once wild corners are taken into production for intensive agriculture.

This pond contains a healthy population of amphibians, including great crested newts, which are nationally rare and so protected. I often stay overnight in my hide to avoid disturbing the snipe and one morning I awoke to the sight of a grey heron snatching a common frog less than five yards away.

The farmer tells me he's seen otters running across nearby grass fields and straight through a paddock – much to the consternation and curiosity of the horses there – to get to this pond for its frogs.

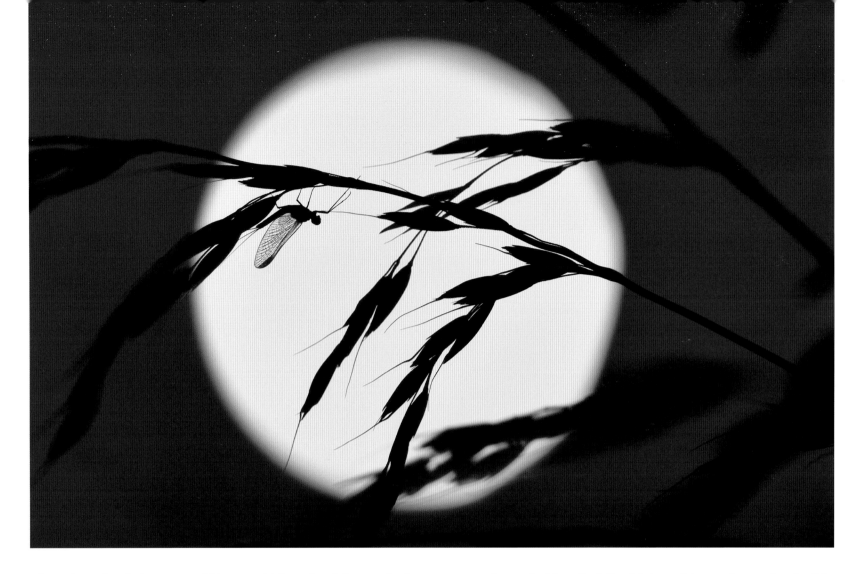

My work involves being out at odd hours, which often means I encounter something unusual or unexpected. I get quite easily sidetracked – something will catch my eye and set me off on an entirely different course to the one on which I set out. So I rarely leave home without packing some equipment for close-ups, just in case. On this occasion, I noticed a mayfly had settled for the night on a single grass stem, so I stayed with it and ended up photographing it silhouetted against a rising full moon before retiring to sleep on the riverbank to await the dawn.

Sometimes on sunny days in spring there's a big hatch and the air is suddenly full of mayflies, gnats and other invertebrates. This bounty provides plenty of food for bats and fledgling birds, and its good news for the fish, too. It results in what fishermen call a 'rise', when the fish feed at the surface. And, in turn, a healthy population of fish means good times for the otters.

Dippers are often my companions on the smaller rivers, as I search and wait for otters. They are handsome birds, sporting shining white bibs and dark brown backs. Dippers breed early, normally building nests in March, and have their first brood away by the end of April. I watched this one and its mate flying back and forth, feeding their young in a dome-shaped nest built on the abutment of a bridge.

They're here all year round, like the king-fishers, but whereas kingfisher numbers fluctu-ate, dropping drastically after hard winters, dippers are more resilient.

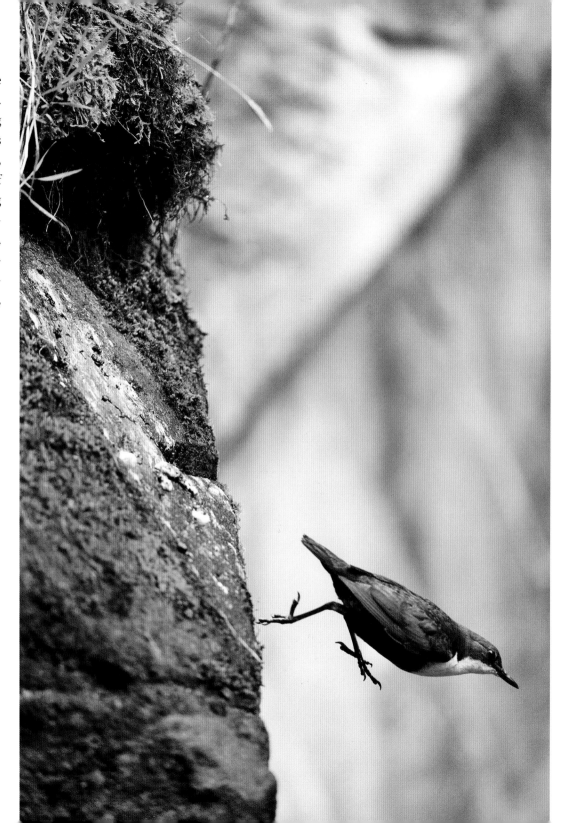

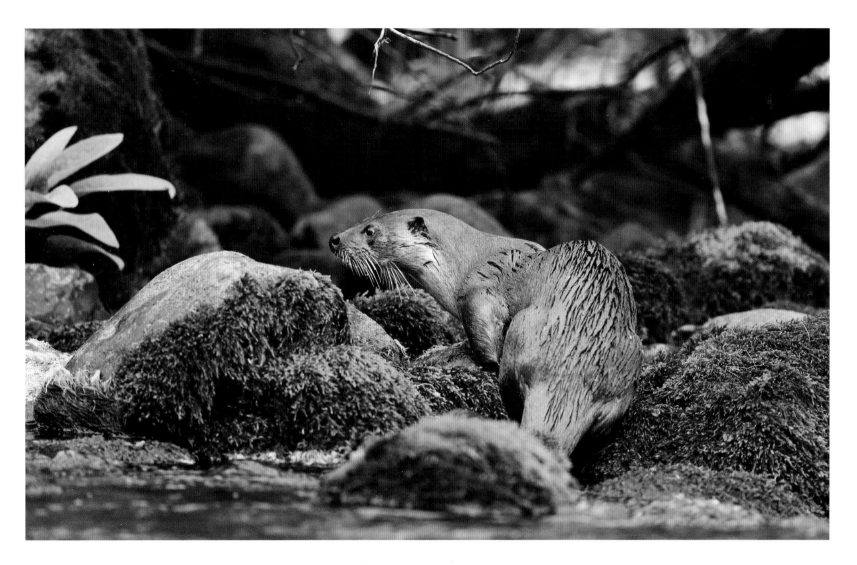

Sometimes I push ahead of an otter I've been following and wait – that's how I captured this photograph of a female coming ashore, early on a May morning, returning to the holt that sheltered her young cub. I had donned a set of neoprene chest waders so that I was able to lie in the chilly river in relative comfort while waiting for her to arrive.

Field guides will tell you that otters can have young in any month of the year, but I've observed a difference between those living in marine environments and those in freshwater habitats, like these. Here, on the rivers, I've consistently seen the first young emerge in late February, whereas on the seashore in the West Highlands and the Hebrides I've tended to first see otter cubs late in the summer, from August to September.

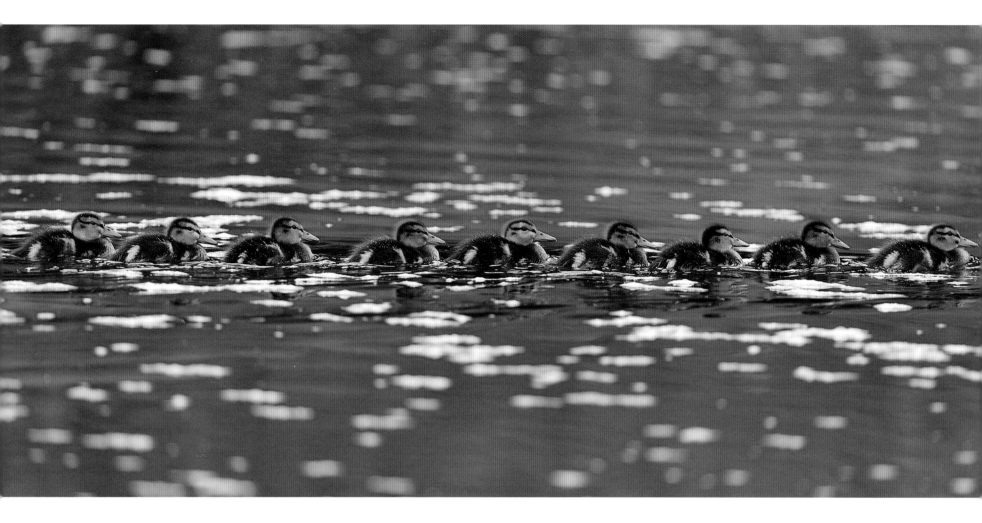

A late brood of ducklings following mum in single file: this was probably the full complement, but their numbers will diminish through the spring. Ducklings are vulnerable to many predators, including herons, crows when on the shore, and otters. Otters do take adult ducks and other waterbirds, but mostly target the young in spring and summer. They will sometimes take ducklings by swimming underneath and snatching them in the water, as well as raiding nests.

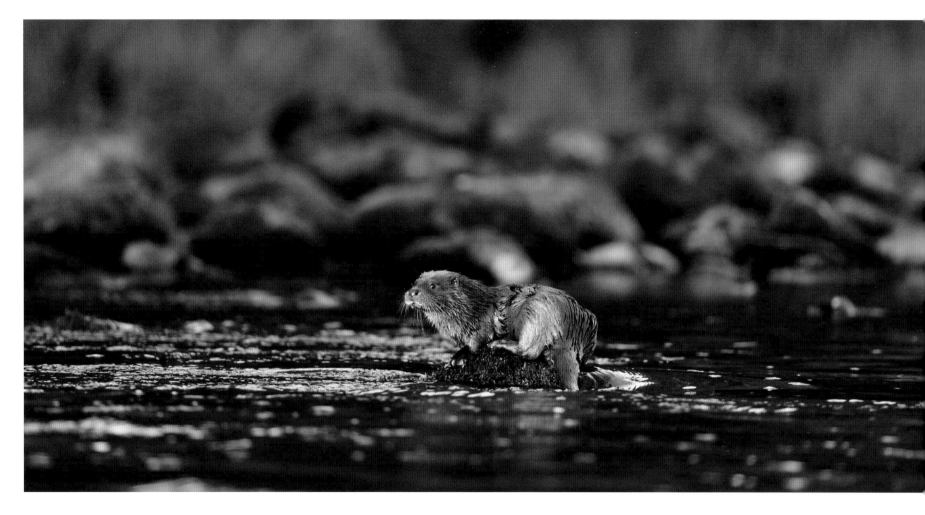

In both marine and river environments, the young otter cubs stay close to mum and make a lot of noise when they get parted. The high-pitched peeping sound of cubs is almost inces-sant when they're small. There are times when I've been looking for otters and have found them purely through sound, hearing these calls. Other times I've slept out on the riverbank and heard otters calling in the darkness, confirming the presence of cubs.

One morning I spotted this cub perched on a rock midstream. It was about half the length of its mother, who was fishing nearby. When-ever the mother disappeared from view for any length of time, the anxious youngster would start calling until she rose up out of the water and edged a little closer to re-assure it.

I watched the pair for over an hour until they retreated to their holt. I was watching from twenty metres away and she knew I was there – but at this distance she tolerated me and made no attempt to move the cub away.

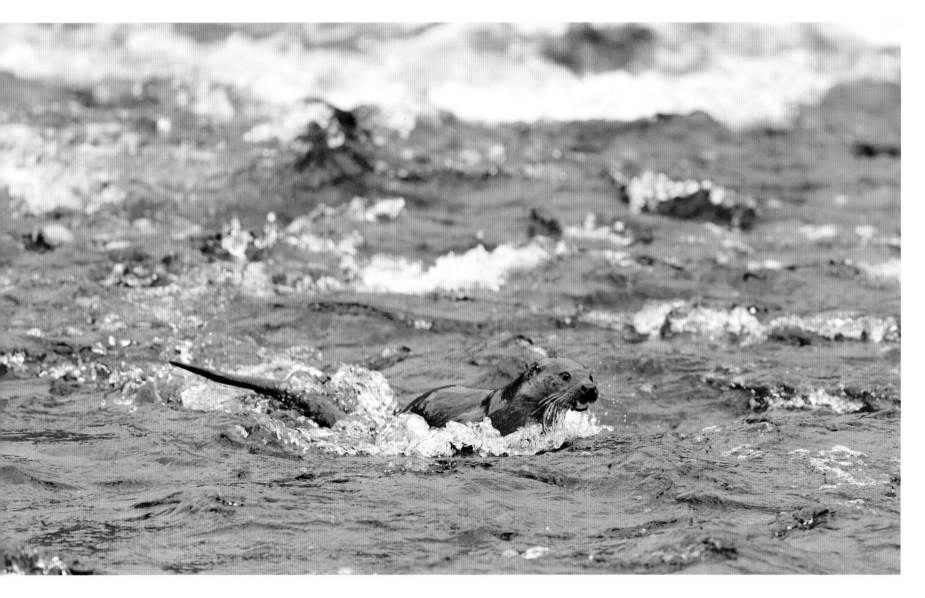

This female was responding to her calling cub. Her whole body seemed intent on reaching it quickly; she propelled herself forward, revealing a sleek outline of glossy muscle.

Otters may have a rather cumbersome, lolloping gait on land, but they are astonishingly graceful and powerful in the water. They are strong, purposeful swimmers, kicking their hind legs together to accelerate, their lithe bodies undulating as they thrust forward.

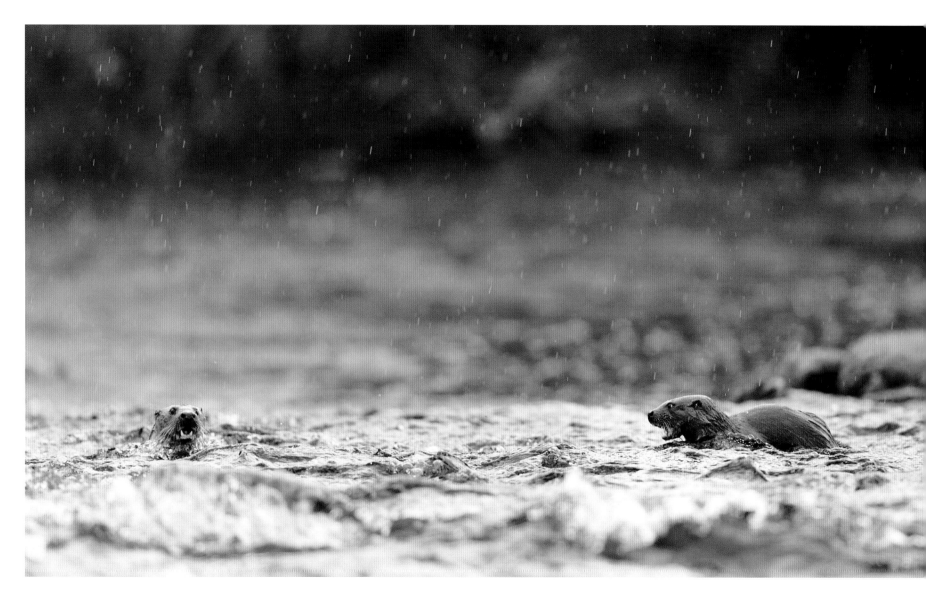

On this rainy morning in May, I watched this mother and cub calling to each other, staying close together as they ventured out hunting.

Female otters raise their cubs without the male, encouraging them into the water and bringing them food until they learn to find and catch it for themselves.

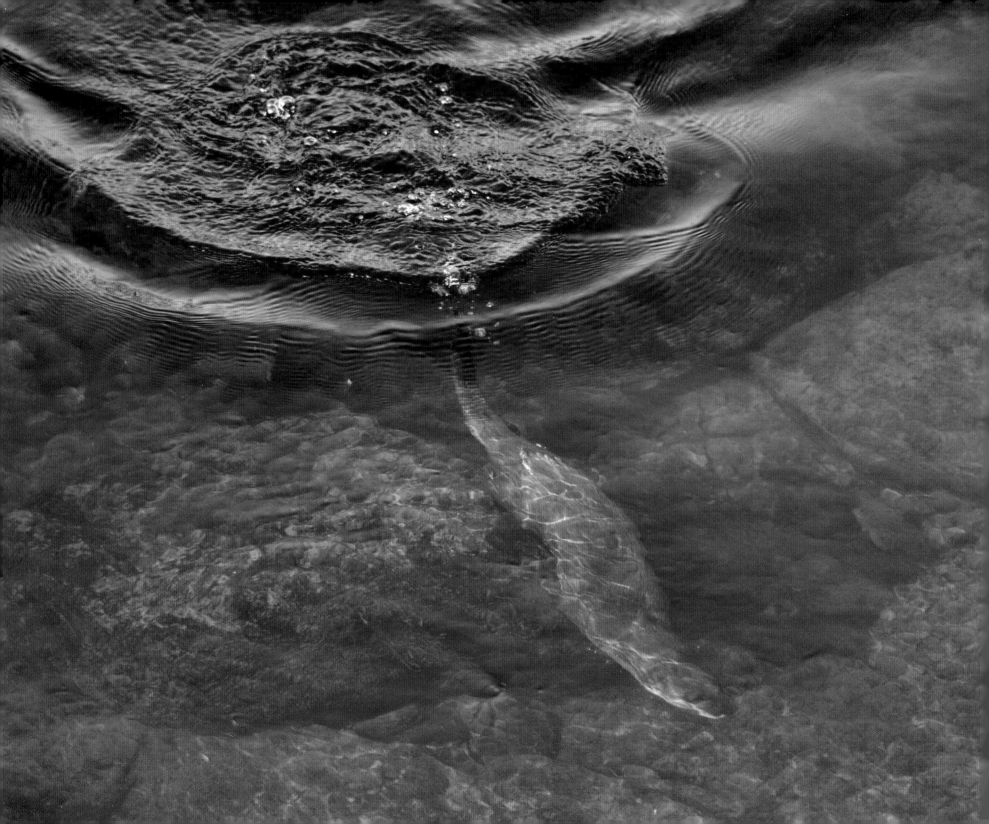

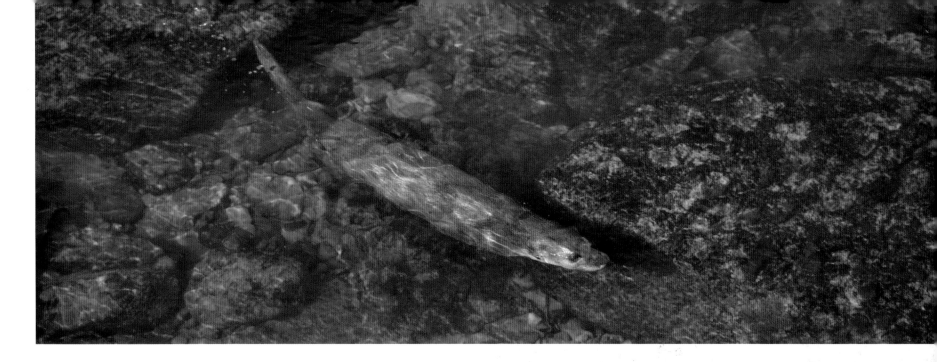

When I'm able to spend time regularly working on the river, I get to know the pattern of the otters' daily movements and therefore have a starting point when I set out to search the river. If I know where the holt is, and see otters going up the river, I know they'll be coming back – what goes upstream must come down! I can then count them out and count them back in again.

This adult female was setting off from her holt one early May evening for a night's fishing and I was leaning over the parapet of a bridge waiting for her. I watched her glide beneath the bridge, swimming through pools of sunlight on the rocky riverbed, her coat gleaming in the light.

Crisp sunlight doesn't offer the easiest of conditions for photographing a subject beneath the water, and I was using a polarising filter on my camera's lens to remove the glare from the surface. Clean, clear water, long after rain, when the sediment has had time to settle and 'flush through', allows the best opportunity to photograph an otter underwater – a fitting way to show an animal so perfectly adapted for an aquatic life in its element.

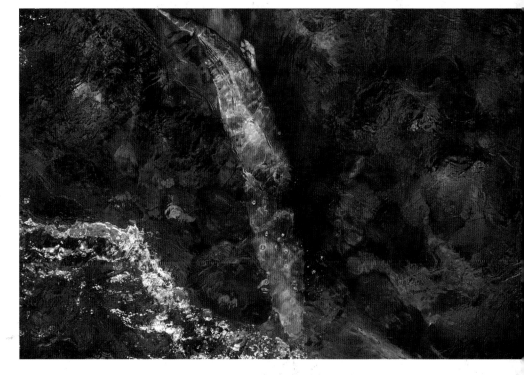

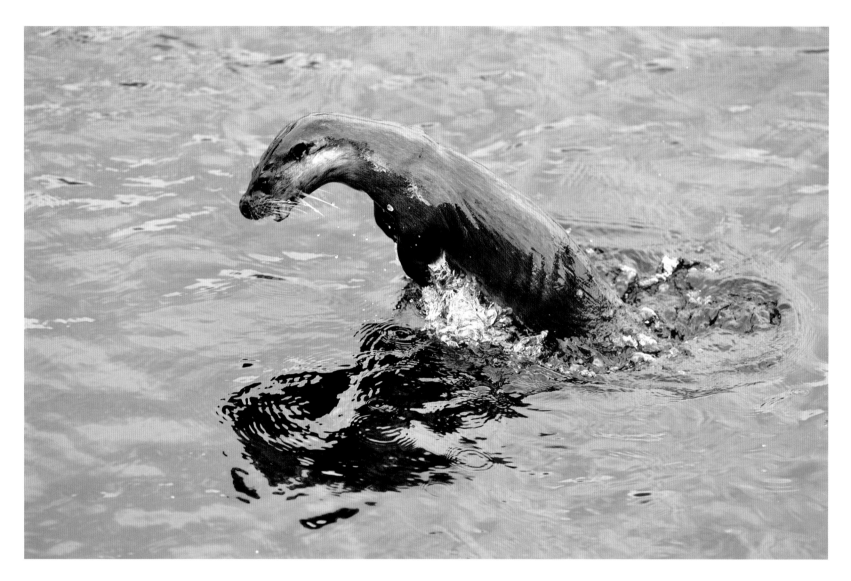

Sometimes the most efficient way of getting to the riverbed is to 'pounce' through the water and so otters thrust themselves upwards to get the trajectory. Diving repeatedly in one small area, this otter was turning over rocks and stones to find small prey hiding beneath, maybe species like stone loaches, which shelter in such places.

Though I've nearly always seen cubs emerge in spring, this well grown youngster was photographed in April and so must have been born in the late summer or autumn of the year before.

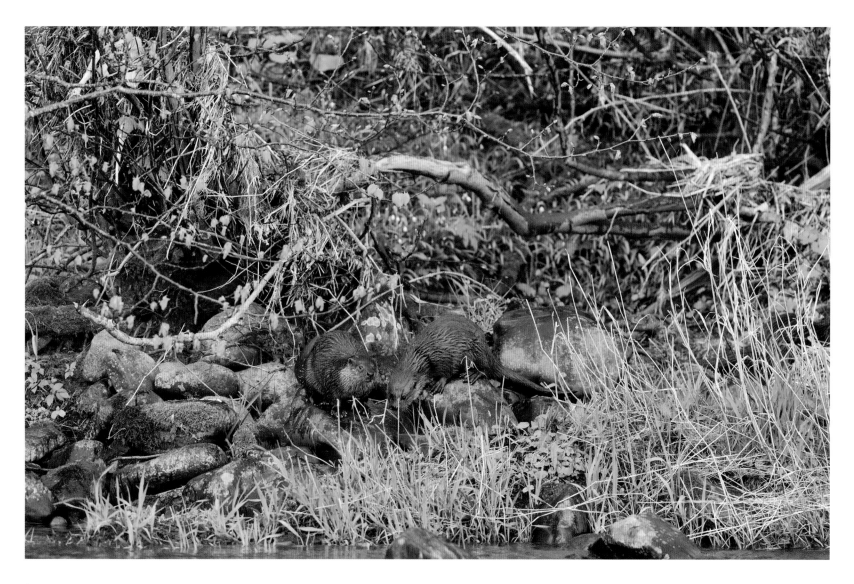

'Getting your eye in' means learning to see otters in the context and camouflage of their environment – small, brown shapes amongst the river and rocks and tangles of branches beside the water.

An hour before sunset one overcast evening in early April, I watched an otter family emerge from their island holt and head downstream. Once the mother got ahead, the three cubs left the river and ran along the bank for about sixty to eighty yards to catch up with her, only pausing for a moment amongst the three-cornered leek in flower and marsh marigolds not yet in bloom before diving in to join her.

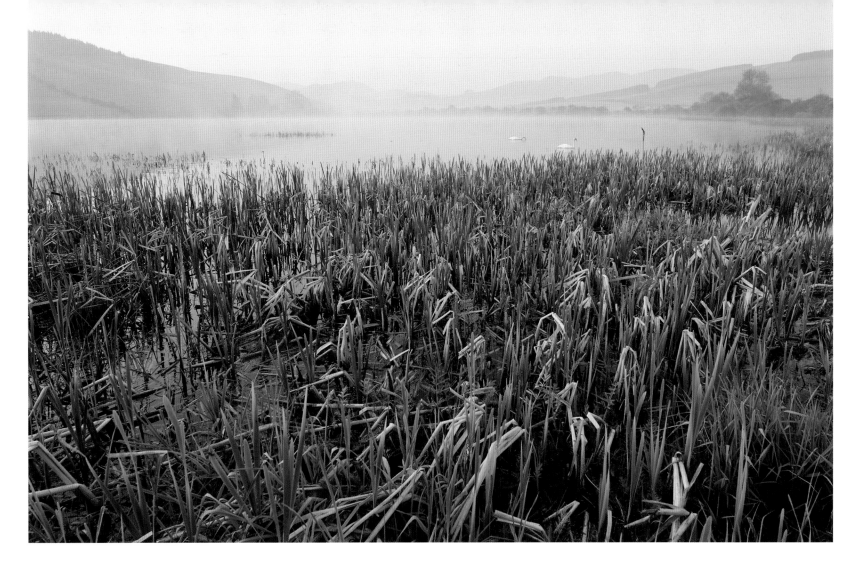

My search for otters takes me not just to rivers but also to inland wetlands. I've spent many a peaceful early morning here at Yetholm Loch, a small inland loch at the edge of the Cheviot Hills managed by the Scottish Wildlife Trust. It's a wonderfully tranquil spot worth visiting at any time of year – in autumn there are greylag and pink-footed geese flying in at dusk, and in springtime sedge warblers and reed buntings are singing away. I haven't had clear views of water rail yet, but I've heard them, and osprey sightings are increasing here, too.

There is an active logbook in the hide, which is invaluable for getting a sense of the recent activity of otters and other wildlife. Records of sightings of otters are invariably accompanied by exclamation marks! Checking the logbook is the first thing I do when I settle into the hide for a comfortable morning, absorbing the beauty and the peace of this place.

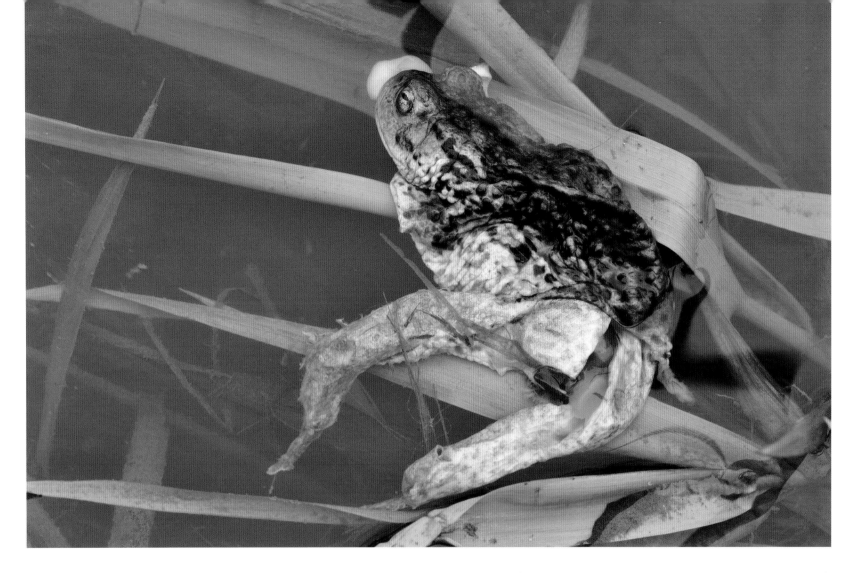

Common toads gather in large congregations for spawning, and otters – ever the opportunists – add them to the spring menu. Toads have poisonous skin glands around the head and neck, which deter most predators, but agile otters have found a way to overcome the tricky business of eating toads. I find the remains of toads that have been caught by otters – they eat the hind legs but 'peel them', leaving the toxic skin behind.

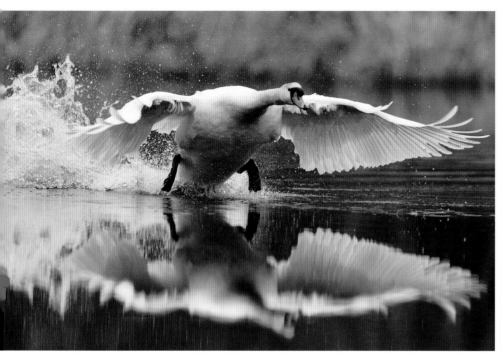

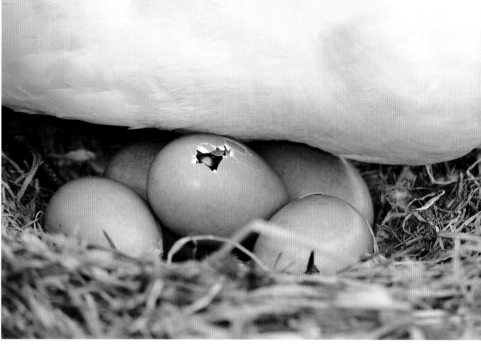

Over winter the mute swans are quite sociable, remaining in groups, but in early spring, in preparation for nesting, they start to disperse, pairing off to select and defend breeding territories. They begin to build their large nest mounds with rushes, grass and vegetation two to three weeks before the eggs are laid.

One day I was out looking for otters and this male swan made its presence known – making a mock charge towards me in an aggressive posture. It only did it once when I first arrived, warning me to keep away from its potential nest site.

I went out to the same site early one May morning in search of otters. At this time of year the dawn comes along before the night has had a chance to get dark, so I was up and settled by the loch at 4.30 a.m.

By seven o'clock, I still hadn't seen an otter and was ready to pack it in for the day and go home for breakfast. Then I came across this pair

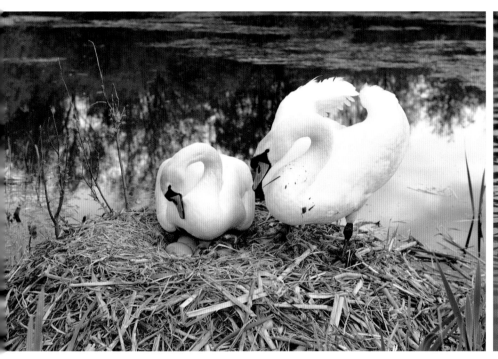 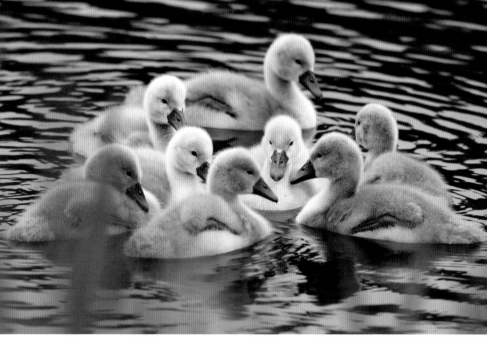

of mute swans on their nest; as I watched, the first egg cracked. The pen (female) became visibly excited as the first straggly cygnet slowly emerged. I settled down to watch and wait until another hatched . . . and then another . . .

It was late in the evening by the time all the eggs had hatched and the eight fluffy cygnets had taken to the water; I'd been there fourteen hours. I got by with my bottle of water, an apple and a Mars bar – 'breakfast' only came when I arrived home that night.

I've been photographing the Tweed's famous herd of mute swans for many years, but this was the first time I'd ever sat and watched a whole brood hatch out – a nice little section of a life story in a day.

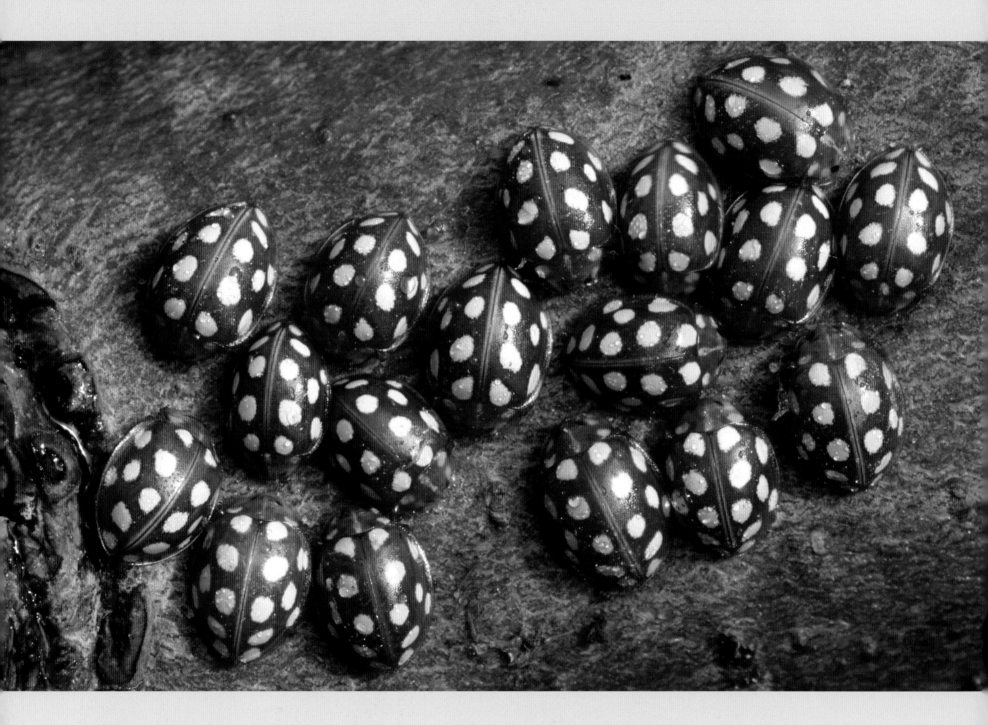

Evening

On a still May evening we head down to meet the River Whiteadder, which curves around the village near Laurie's home. It's a short drive but packed full of information; it seems there's a wildlife story for every twist and turn in the road. He shows me the corner where once he stood in the dark watching pipistrelle bats, learning how many thousandths of a second of flash duration it took to capture their darting flight. Over there are the fields where brown hare, grey partridge, barn owl or woodcock were photo-graphed, from hides built all around surrounding farmland.

We leave the car and wade through a mass of three-cornered leek flowers, which cover the wooded slopes down to the river, scenting the evening air. Two roe deer are grazing; they startle and bound away as we approach, leaving glimpses of white rumps as they disappear through the trees. Laurie continues his softly spoken commentary, naming the plants and the bird calls, explaining that this secret place tucked into the river valley has a microclimate all of its own. He points out the striped hairs that show where badgers have been scratching. We pass by the ash trees where he photographed the orange ladybirds that cluster in their hundreds each winter on the shady north side of the olive-grey tree trunks.

The soft mud by the water's edge forms a perfect mould: it's just wet enough to hold the story of its recent visitors, dry enough not to smudge the prints: the two slots of roe deer; the wider pads of badger, with straight rows of four forward-facing toes; and – what we are searching for – the five rounded, webbed pads of otter. They're here.

Laurie points to a moss-covered log nearby – it holds a squidge of oily black otter spraint. We crouch down to examine the spraint through a hand lens, looking for the white glint of fish scales – it's moist, and so otters have been here recently.

Silently, we follow the loop of the river, Laurie striding ahead. He walks like a predator, lifting his feet and placing them down, soft and deliberate as a big cat – a leopard perhaps, all senses alert, scanning around, taking everything in, listening, feeling the direction of the wind. Laurie carries a tripod over one shoulder and a heavy bag of photographic kit on the other, but he glides along totally unencumbered by it all, ducking under branches and moving through dense vegetation, stepping over fences, always off the beaten path.

We stop suddenly. 'There,' says Laurie quietly, and my eyes dart to the water, scanning for otters, but it's a kingfisher – an iridescent streak of brilliant turquoise and just a moment of russet. It's startlingly bright, the colours incongruous against the soft greys and browns and muted greens of rock, river, mud and trees.

We settle a while on the riverbank, watching. The water stays bright, as the sky around us darkens. In the stillness, silver rings appear on the surface as trout rise, making me start, as does movement on the water upstream, but Laurie has clocked it all in his peripheral vision and doesn't stir – it's just the clumsy bow wave of a passing duck, not the streamlined 'v' of an otter's wake. The wind's behind us, he says, so there's not much chance of a sighting; the otters are still shy here, where nobody much goes. But he points out the kestrel roost over on the cliffs and the places where Daubenton's bats skim low over the water. A tawny owl calls.

Much of the land around here has been tamed by years of intensive agriculture, but where the river twists through these steep-sided cliffs there are remnants of natural woodland and a rich, wild habitat. As we head home through the almost-dark, Laurie points to where roe deer have nipped the emerging buds of the butterbur flowers. Such an in-depth knowledge of habitat, he says, is the reward you get for working so close to home.

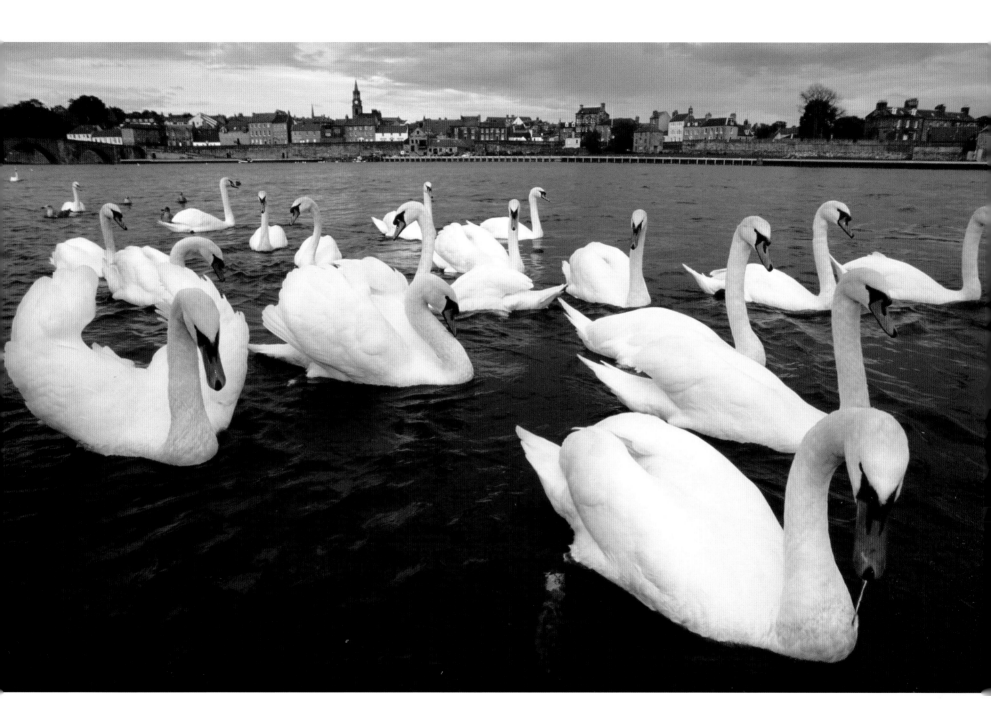

Chapter 2　Home Beat

Laurie can't remember when his interest in the natural world began; it has simply always been there. Children are naturally curious, always picking things up, collecting, exploring, questioning. Laurie simply didn't grow out of it. He describes his parents as interested, though not expert, but times were different then, children had more freedom to explore outside, and the natural world was closer. There were chores to be done on his father's allotment, fishing trips with his grandfather, family outings to collect rosehips, field mushrooms, brambles and conkers.

The family lived in the centre of Berwick-upon-Tweed, close to the river. From a very young age, Laurie would set out alone, walking for miles along the riverside, exploring, observing, building dens, driven by a restless energy and an intense curiosity – always wondering what was round the next corner. At school he

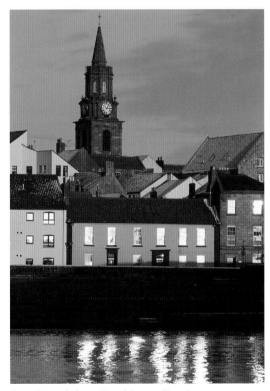
Opposite and above: Berwick-upon-Tweed.

paid attention to biology and nature study, fascinated by the interconnections of the natural world. Inspired by Gerald Durrell books and armed with an array of *Observer's* books and other natural history guides, he began his life-long study of Scotland's wildlife and wild places, focusing on his own native habitat of Berwickshire. There was a lifetime's work for an explorer right here – with rivers and woods, farmland, moor and coast. He looked carefully at each little piece of the jigsaw of habitats and began to see how it all fitted together, how each bit affected the others; how it changed.

Family holidays camping in the Highlands and Islands provided inspirational glimpses into the wild beauty of Scotland's more rugged landscapes. In those days, it was a big deal to see a buzzard on a telegraph pole on the Isle of Mull. On a particularly memorable trip to the remote shores of Argyll's Ardnamurchan Peninsula,

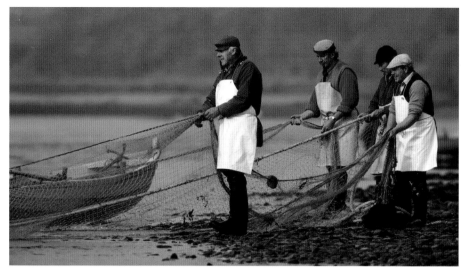

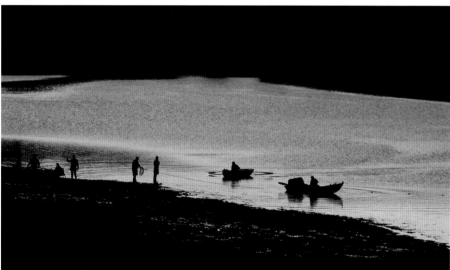

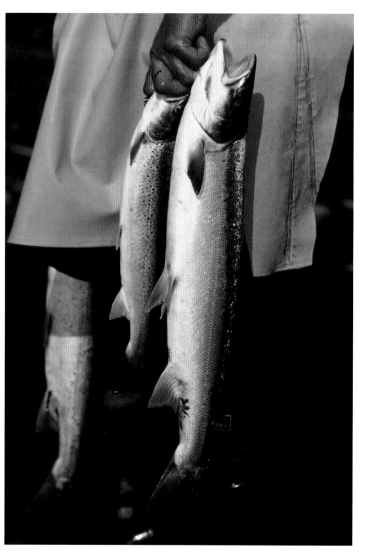

Known as 'net and cobble' this ancient style of fishing was still a familiar sight when I was young.

Laurie looked down and saw a 'something' in the water and realised it wasn't a seal. The something looped and rolled in the turquoise sea and disappeared with a flick of a tapered tail: it was his first sighting of an otter.

As a schoolboy Laurie was already going to lengths others didn't go to – walking further, staying up later, waiting longer. As a result, he witnessed events that others rarely saw – the heavy grace of herons flying in to roost in a field

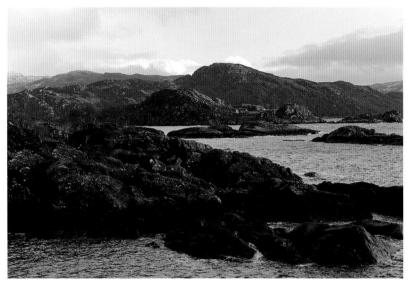

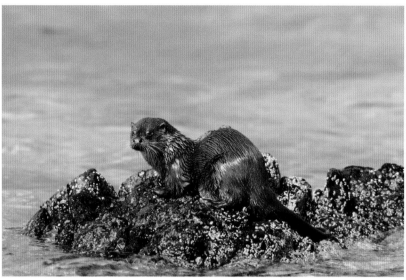

The exact location where I saw my first wild otter from the shore of Loch Sunart, Ardnamurchan on a childhood holiday in the 1960s.

I returned years later to take this, my first publishable photograph of a wild otter.

at dawn, gatherings of over-wintering long-eared owls roosting in a blackthorn thicket on the riverside; badger cubs first emerging from their setts. Even then he saw the magic in tiny transient moments, ones others might have missed – the gleam of sunlight on birch bark, raindrops on an upturned oak leaf.

He moved like a shaman between the mundane world of school and home, and the enchanted realm of the riverside. But he wanted to bring something back. He was thrilled by his experiences but frustrated by his attempts to share them with others: neither drawing nor talking could adequately convey what he had witnessed or why it was so special. The solution came from his grandmother, who presented the twelve-year-old boy with the gift of an insta-matic camera from Boots. He remembers the moment vividly – opening the box, its fluores-cent dayglo green inset holding a small camera, a roll of film and some flash cubes. He took to it immediately; this was the medium he'd been looking for, to tell the stories of his adventures. But he soon recognised the camera's limitations: when attempting to photograph mute swans and frogspawn, he couldn't get the camera to realise the pictures in his mind's eye.

Laurie was lucky to have receptive relatives nearby: his maternal aunt Maureen was an artist and botanist, living in Edinburgh and exploring the jungles of Borneo in search of new species of rhododendrons. Her husband Colin

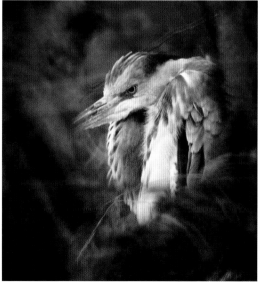

From 1975, the style of this grey heron image – taken through vegetation – was a landmark for me.

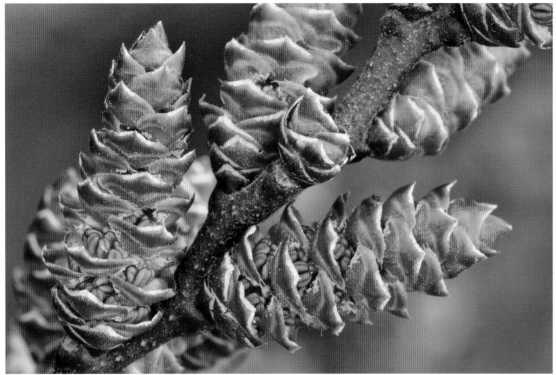

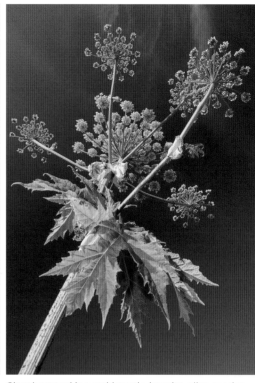

The scent of bog myrtle epitomizes the Highlands to me. When I lead photography workshops there I enjoy crushing some between my fingers and introducing people to the sweet, resinous aroma.

Giant hogweed is a problematic, invasive, alien species – but also photogenic.

was a professional photographer working at Edinburgh's Royal (Dick) School of Veterinary Studies. They shared Laurie's interest in nature, his sense of exploration and his artist's eye, and they recognised his talent. Colin gave the schoolboy an SLR camera and a couple of lenses: the tools he needed to take the next steps. And Laurie took them in great leaps, quickly finding his own voice by experimenting, pushing at boundaries, always looking for a different angle. He rolled his own black-and-white film from thirty-metre rolls, converted a large dog kennel in his grandparents' garden into a darkroom and used a Russian-made enlarger to produce prints. His family still remember them drying all over the house. He wanted pictures with stories to tell, and to find a new way to tell them: by sitting up a tree all night on a plank, or getting down low for a frog's eye view of the water.

When Laurie left school, his interest in animals led him to a job as a keeper at Edinburgh Zoo. He brought his camera with him and his employers were happy for him to spend his lunchtimes taking pictures of the kangaroos and capybaras in their cages, which he sold in the zoo shop. But his real interest was in wild creatures in their natural habitat. While living in Edinburgh, he would spend his weekends taking long walks in wild places, back home in Berwickshire or along the East Lothian coastline. The nature reserve at Aberlady Bay was a favourite haunt, with its special light, rich habitats and vast flocks of wintering geese. He would walk for miles, photographing whatever captured his interest and imagination: expansive

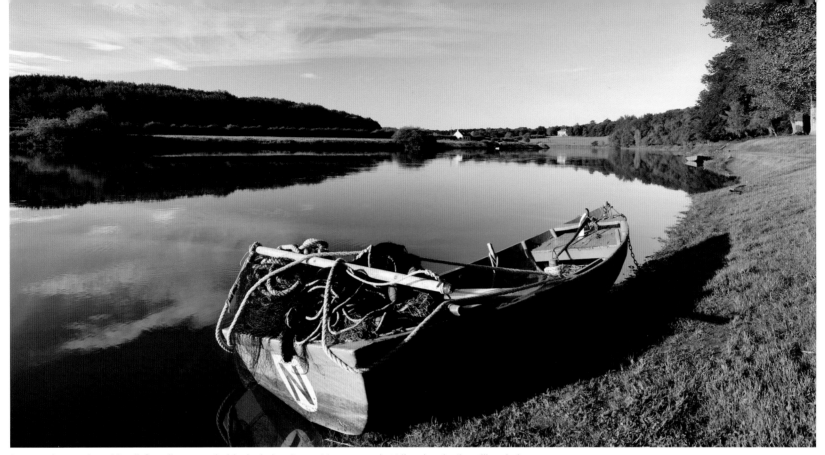

In my early teens I would walk for miles to reach this site below Paxton House; now that I live close by, I'm still exploring.

seascapes or dense tunnels of sea buckthorn, and once even a sea mouse, a marine worm with fur-like spines of iridescent blue and green.

Guided again by his aunt and uncle, Laurie left the zoo to embark on a photography degree at Edinburgh's Napier University. In his four years there, he never met another 'wannabe nature photographer'. There were courses on architecture, interiors, portraiture . . . Nature was barely a genre, then. But he adapted assignments to suit his own quest – such as using an exercise with an old large-format studio camera

to photograph a great-spotted woodpecker, or creating an audio-visual slideshow from the wildlife of Aberlady Bay.

Laurie had known before he began his degree that he wanted to be a nature photographer, and the course only confirmed this and equipped him with the technical skills to further his craft. And he knew his place wasn't among caged animals or in the classroom but out there in the wild, exploring and observing at his own pace in his own way. He knew where he was heading but had to find a route to making the

life he wanted a viable reality. He found stepping stones: a stint as a wine waiter in a boardroom, a gruelling winter working in medieval conditions in a maltings factory, two years as a medical photographer. Then he took the plunge to see if he could make a living doing what he'd always done: exploring ever further into the wild world, capturing fleeting moments of natural light on wild beauty, and bringing them back to show and to share.

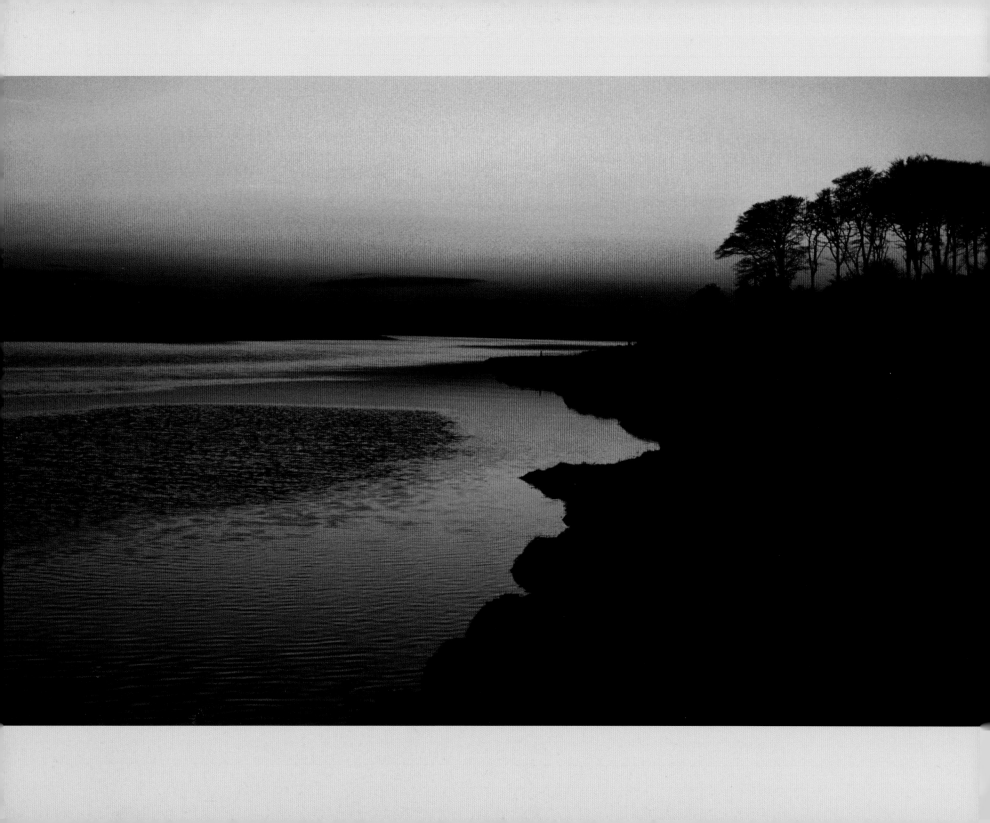

New Road

In June, we walk the path along the north bank of the Tweed, known locally as the 'New Road', which follows the river out of town. It leads us from the centre of Berwick-upon-Tweed, a stone's throw from the house where Laurie was born, and the house and garages his grandfather built, then under the three bridges that span the bright river, and on and on upstream.

Today the river is brilliant blue and picturesque, with the town's rowing club out in force on the water and groups of elegant mute swans drifting by. But we're walking through layers of time, our route punctuated by the locations of photographs and memories of wild encounters. Laurie has walked this path and known this river all his life.

As we set out, Laurie parts the dense ivy that falls like a curtain over the rocks by the riverbank, revealing the secret space behind, where a boy could watch from a natural hide. We pass the ruins of the thirteenth-century castle and note the crevice in the eroded sandstone of the rock where Laurie used to see tiny wrens roosting at night, huddled together for shelter. Further along is a cottage with no road or track to it. It's always been occupied, and the lights in the windows would give some orientation as he walked home in the darkness after long hours of badger watching. On some dark nights he was spooked by strange gasps carried on the wind from the water, until he realised it was the breath of grey seals that had followed the salmon up the river.

When you've known a landscape so long, you see it in layers of what is and what used to be. There's a field beside a stream that was once a rich marshy wetland, bright with irises and marsh marigolds and dragonflies; there were swathes of watercress on the banks and water voles in the burn. Laurie explains that when they built the Berwick bypass in the early 1970s, the land was filled in with spoil from nearby road cuttings, bringing this living, marshy world to an abrupt end. It was Laurie's first awareness that his outdoor playground was threatened – something darker and duller was encroaching from the world beyond.

A few miles upriver we scramble up a nettle-covered grassy bank. There's a large beech here, with some planks attached about ten-metres high, across a fork in the tree. It's the remains of a hide that Laurie built more than thirty years ago to get level with a kestrel's nest on an old oak just below it. We sit in the sun looking up at it and remembering. He explains how he used to spend eight or ten hours at a time up there, watching the kestrels coming and going, waiting for the right moment in just the right light to get the photograph he wanted.

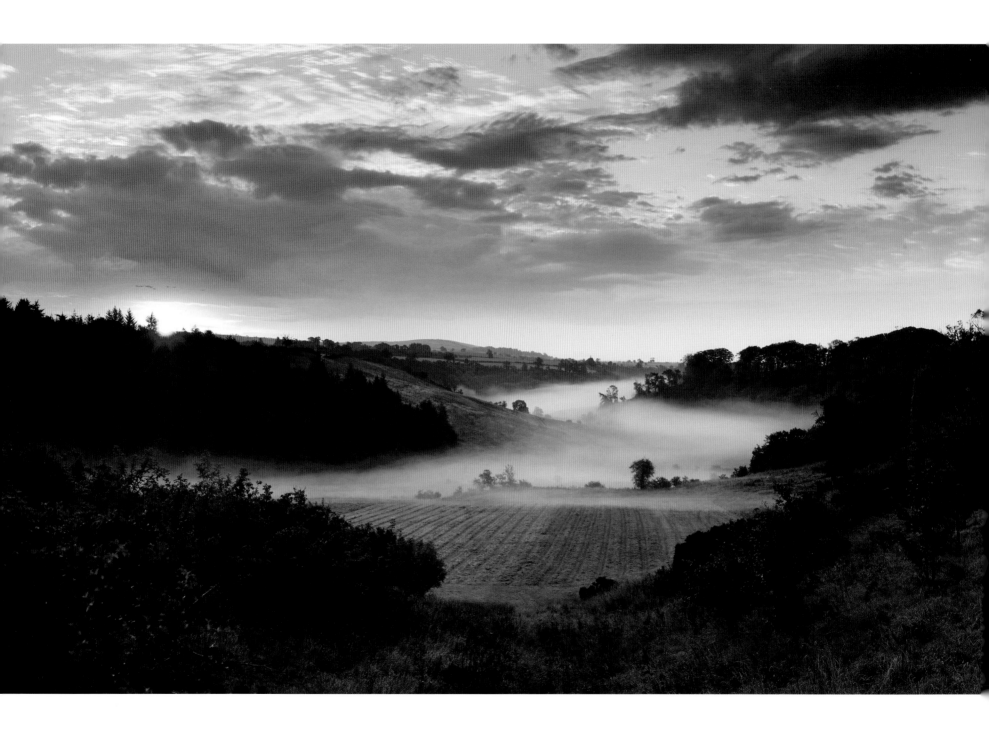

Chapter 3 Summer

Summer is the season when the plant kingdom claims the riverbank for itself, forming walls of brilliant green between the bank-side paths and the river. The trees are rich and resplendent, and beneath there's a vibrant jungle of comfreys, nettles and mints, with bursts of frothy meadowsweet, magenta spikes of purple loosestrife and the pinks of flowering rushes.

In some areas the large, invasive species dominate. Huge stands of Japanese knotweed, Himalayan balsam and giant hogweed can render parts of the riverbank virtually impenetrable in summer. This makes life difficult for walkers, anglers and nature photographers trying to get to the river, but I suspect that the dense shelter is ideal habitat for an otter to lie up in and safely snooze in peace. So the otters – out and about now, with growing cubs – are less dependent on their holts for shelter and 'bivvy out' more, making a couch in the vegetation by the riverside.

The birdlife on the river has calmed after the crescendo of spring and it's quieter now, but people are out in force – there are ramblers and anglers, dog walkers and joggers on the bank-side paths. The abundance of light in summer means the opportunities for otter spotting begin long before most people are awake and stretch long into the evenings. Dawn comes so early that you're almost better off to bivvy out too, waking on the riverbank ready and waiting to catch otters in the early morning light.

When I'm out and about, I'm sometimes torn between the need to get to where I'm going and the urge to stop and photograph things along the way. I'm very easily distracted, but that's also how I get some of the best photographs, so I have to find a balance there somewhere!

I try to cherry-pick these days – filtering out subjects that I have in my image library already and selectively seeking out scenes or species I haven't got, or that I want to improve on. But there are moments when I see something and simply *have* to pause and photograph it, to capture the moment. I can't just walk past.

This was very early on a summers' morning, as I was heading down to the river to look for otters. It's a safe bet going out at that time of day: the odds of a sighting – whether of otters or other wildlife – increase just by being out when animals are more active and fewer people are around. I favour sunrise over sunset – it's quieter on the riverbank and there are magical effects, like the mist rising and hanging like a veil over the long snake of the river as the cool night becomes a warm day. It's not easy to get up and out at that time, but that's the reward!

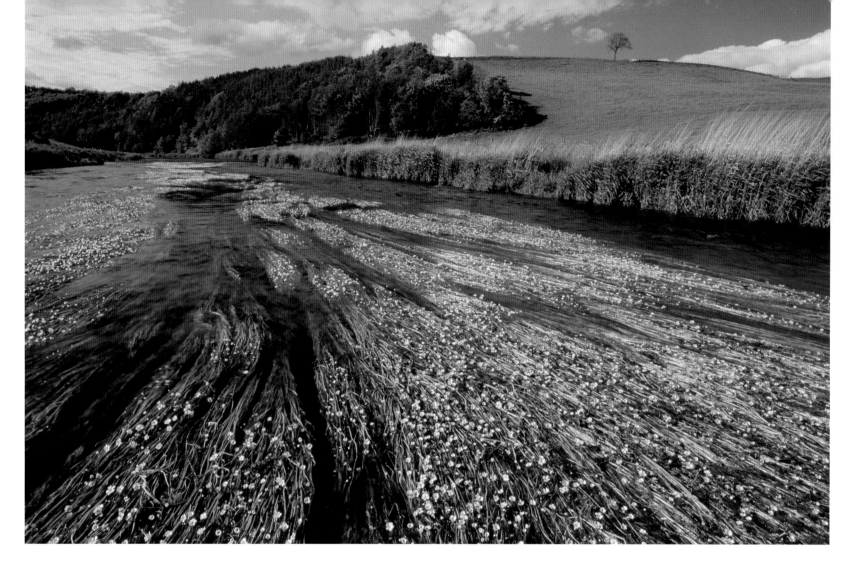

This is the River Whiteadder, which stems from the Lammermuir Hills and swings round the village where I live on its way to meet the Tweed. It's a beautiful river, with very good quality water. I see a lot of this plant, river water crowfoot (*Ranunculus fluitans*), lying like long, green, flowing streamers in the water, holding up its little white flowers to the sky. It needs clear, clean, oxygen-rich water and so its presence can be an indicator of the health of the wider environment, like lichens in the western oakwoods. It provides food, cover and habitat for fish and invertebrate life, and it flourishes in healthy, shallow rivers. I was standing in the middle of the Whiteadder in order to capture this, having taken off my boots, rolled up my trouser legs and paddled in – I've been caught out too many times, bending down to take a photo in the river and water flooding in over the tops of my wellingtons.

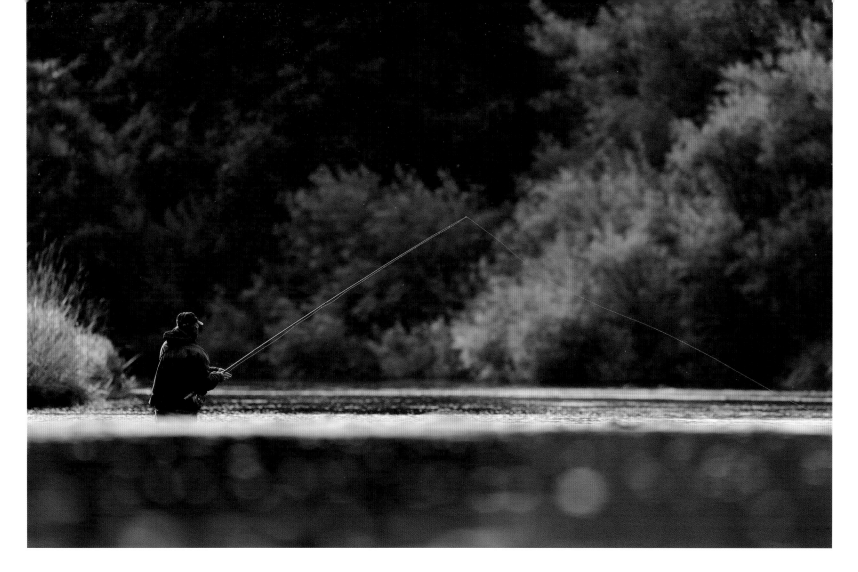

I wanted to capture an otter's-eye view of an angler, portraying the sense of how people on the river are being watched and monitored by otters, even if they don't know the animals are there.

I glean sightings tips from anyone who spends time on the water. As anglers are engaged in an activity that involves standing still in the river for long periods, they have a far greater chance of seeing otters than most dog walkers on the riverside paths.

There's a longstanding running battle between water bailiffs and poachers on the Tweed and to either side I could look like the opposition! So it's best that they both know what I'm up to. They are good sources of otter information, both being out on the river at odd hours.

In the places I go regularly, anglers, walkers, bailiffs, poachers and dog walkers alike all know what I'm about and will go out of their way to update me about otter sightings. They're all river folk, and we compare notes on what we have seen.

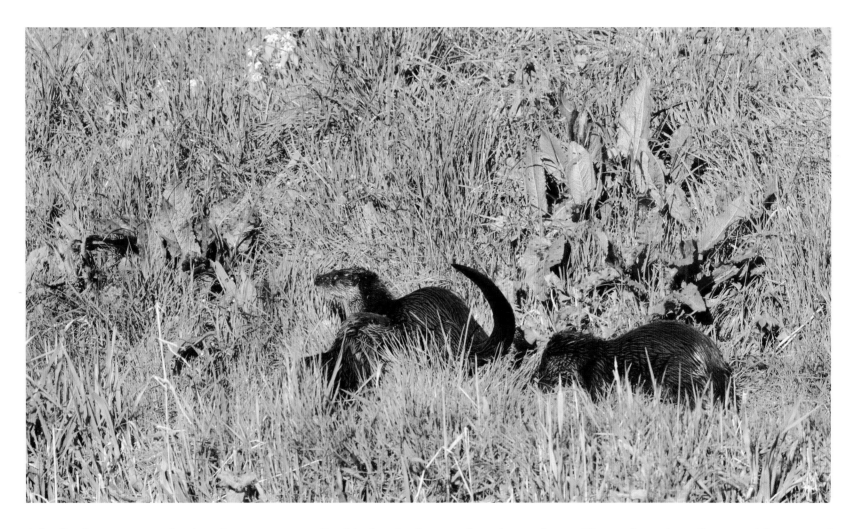

A family of otters out together in early summer, travelling along, alternating between the riverbank and the water. On the riverbank, the mother is lifting her tail and sprainting, the cub following behind, learning how to patrol their territory.

By this time in the year, the cubs are far more confident: they're still out with Mum, but they're getting older and bolder and becoming more independent as they perfect their fishing skills. There's a lot less 'contact calling' between the mother and the cubs by this stage – the cubs will stray for quite a distance without any of them seeming worried.

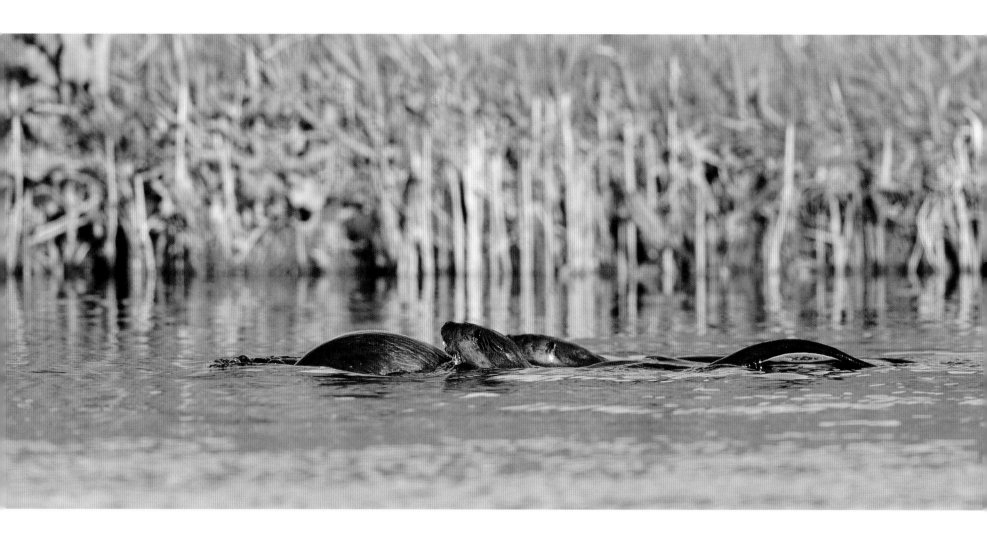

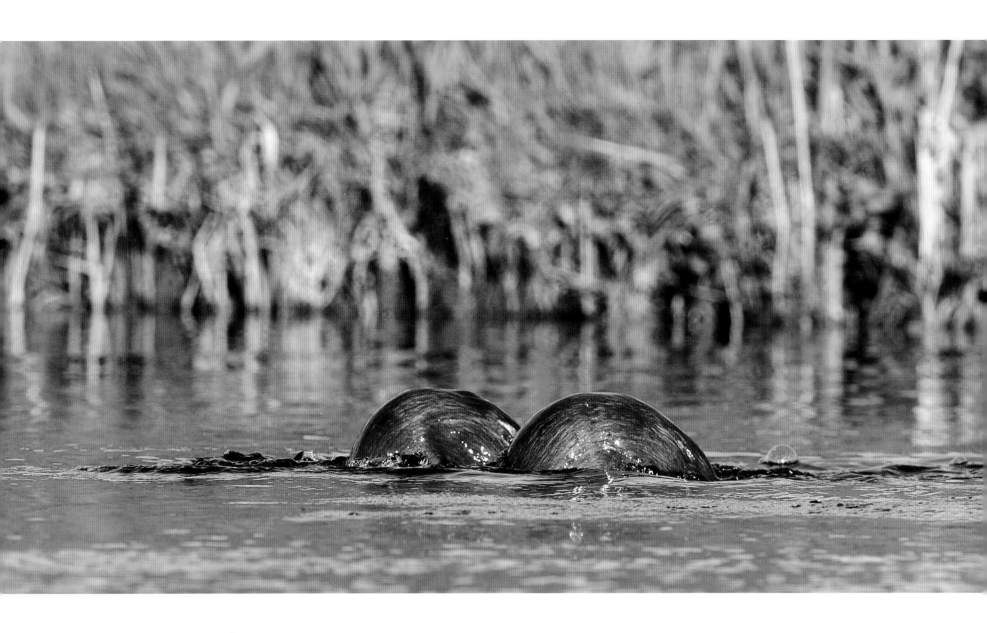

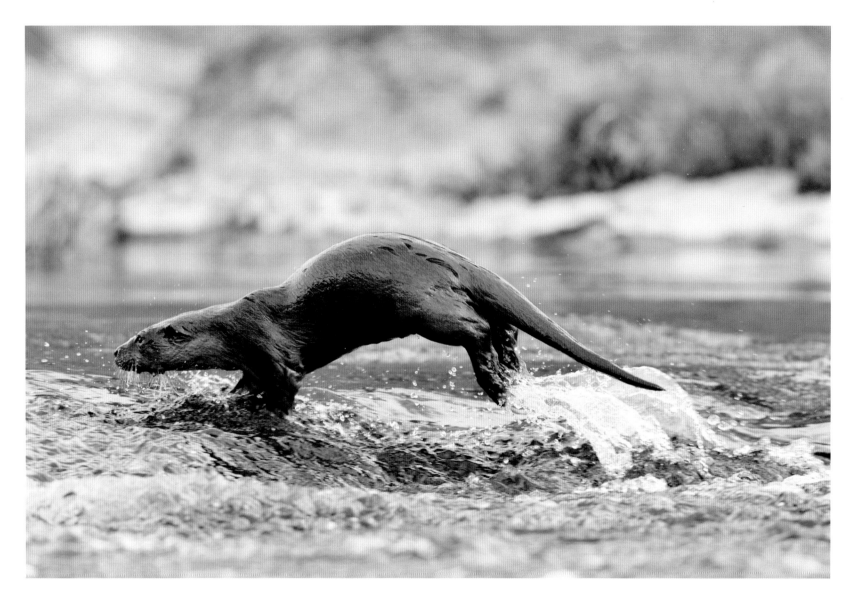

When the river levels are low in summer, the otters – once they've fed well – will travel in a distinctive manner up the edges of the river as they head back to their holts. They seem to bound over the water, running over rocks or other obstacles, and for me it's an ideal opportunity to photograph the whole animal, something that is hard to capture in the winter. I stake out the spots where they have to leave the water when travelling, where there are rocks or shelves underneath.

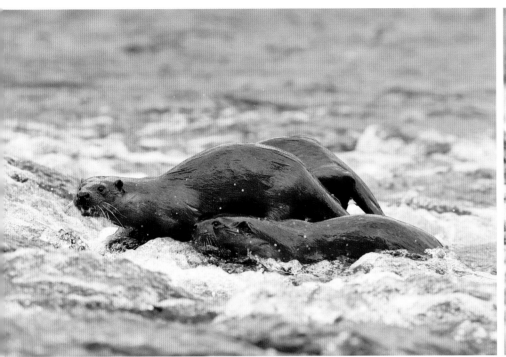 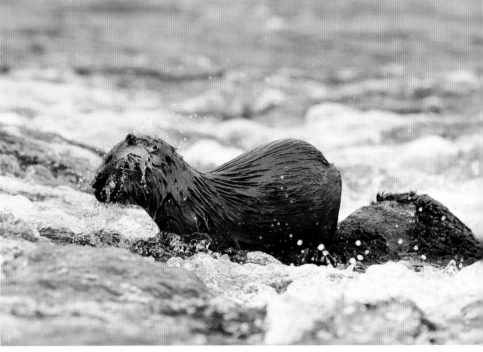

I watched this family leaving their holt, which was among roots and woody debris in the bows of a small island in the middle of the river. They set off to fish and seemed to be working as a group, all milling around the same areas. When water levels are low on the rivers, the otters will target small waterfalls and areas of rough water such as small weirs or where a rock shelf creates a step in the river. These areas seem more productive and they probably find it easier to corner fish in such places.

Later they were travelling back upstream towards their holt, still picking things up along the way, browsing and snacking. I had watched them from first light, and the last I saw was an otter disappearing into the back of the island at 8 a.m. It was the end of a long encounter.

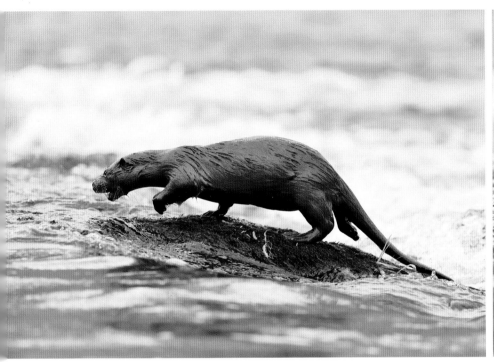
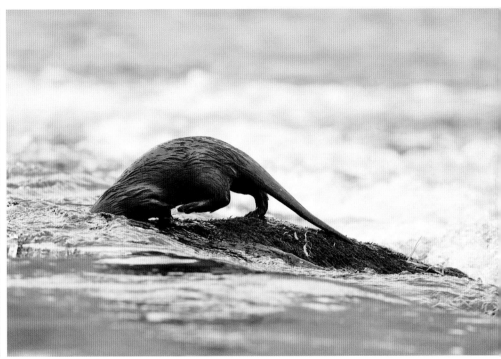

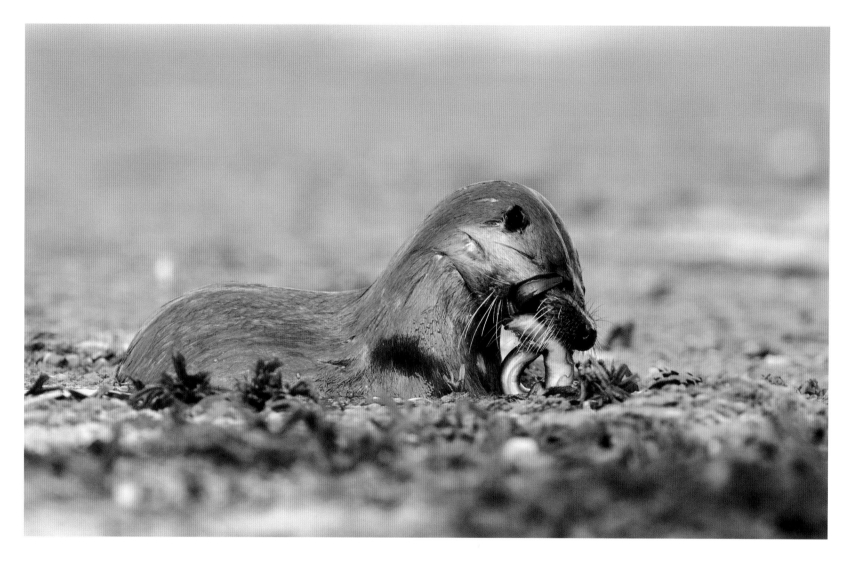

In its lower reaches, the Tweed changes character: it's tidal and brackish and strewn with seaweed. I was watching early one July morning in Berwick-upon-Tweed, just by the Royal Border Bridge, which carries the railway over the mouth of the river, when I spotted an otter at a distance. It was hunting eels, a favourite food and a summer treat. The tide was going out, leaving just gravel bed and mud either side of the river channel, and so I was working in a completely flat landscape, with no cover to hide behind. I ran forward when the otter dived, a technique I'd practised while photographing otters in the Highlands and Islands. Then I was on my hands and knees, crawling commando-style to home in closer when the otter came ashore. This day I got lucky, having got myself into a position reasonably close to where the

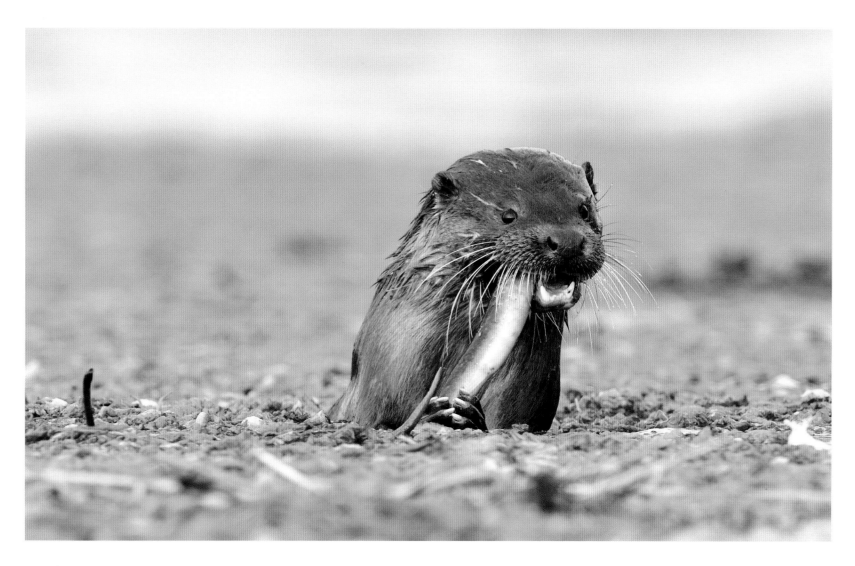

otter happened to land a large eel and was busy trying to subdue its writhing, wriggling, slippery prey.

Afterwards the otter continued on up-stream, still hunting eels, but it didn't catch anything big enough to have to bring ashore. I watched as it was mobbed by black-headed gulls. These birds are such opportunists, I see them going after the grey seals when the seals are feeding on spent salmon in the estuary, waiting for their chance to grab titbits, but I don't think they stood much chance of grabbing any of the eel from the otter. I stayed watching for a long time, but the opportunities for photography were diminishing rapidly, as the morning was becoming a hot day and the bright light was creating too much contrast.

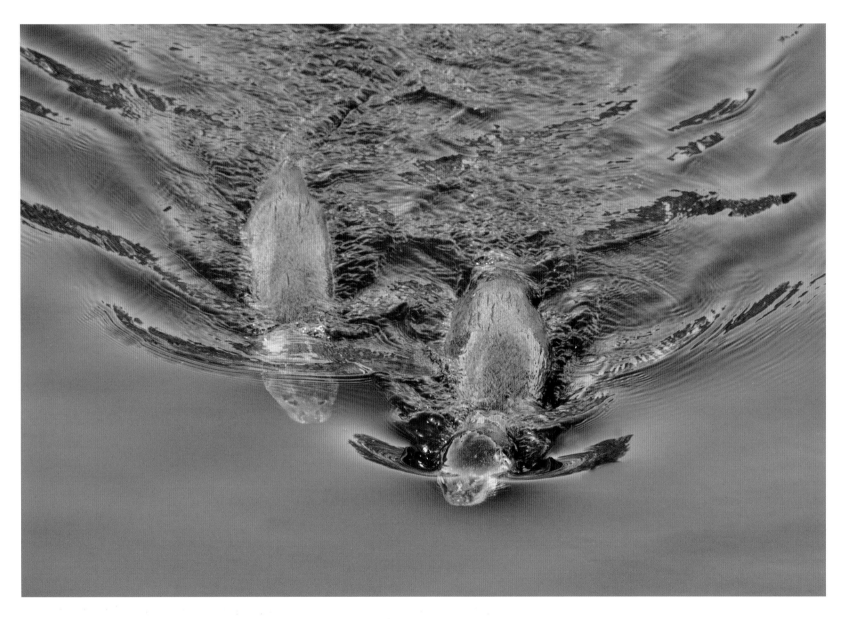

Two grown otter cubs travelling close together as they return to their holt after fishing. I was up on a bridge as they swam underneath, the penetrating light making the animals more visible underwater and also reflecting the blues and greens of the summer above. Seeing the otters' faces so clearly gave me the idea that it would be possible to photograph them through the water in the right conditions.

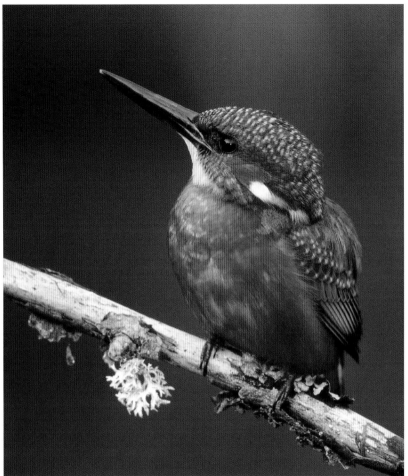 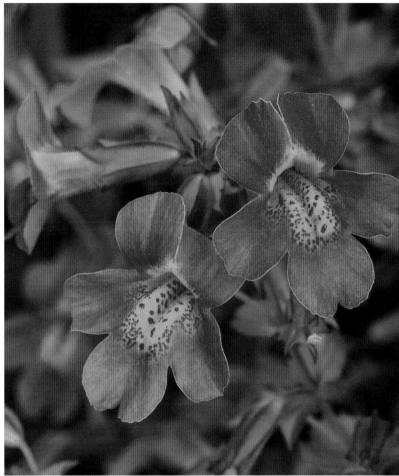

Kingfishers were one of the reasons I made the transition from black-and-white film to colour. Back in the early days when I was working at Edinburgh zoo, I was home one weekend taking photographs of grey herons on the Tweed when a kingfisher landed on a perch right in front of my hide. Seeing its brilliant colours it just made no sense to photo-graph it in black and white. These jewel-like birds are reasonably common on the Tweed. You can't miss them once you've tuned into their high-pitched, whistling call and their low, fast flight over the water.

This colourful monkey flower (*Mimulus sp.,*) is another introduced species that has natu-ralised and spread along the watercourses. The Tweed valley is a farmed landscape and always will be – it's a rich fertile plain that will always be needed for food production. But the rivers wind through this landscape, forming wildlife-rich corridors, along which plants and animals travel.

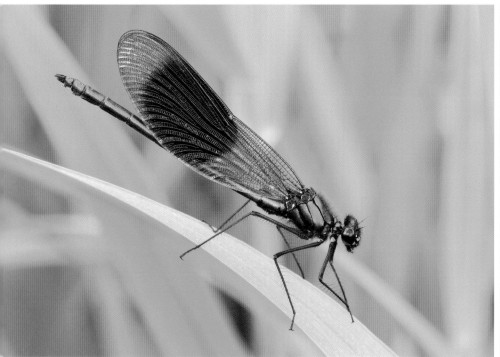 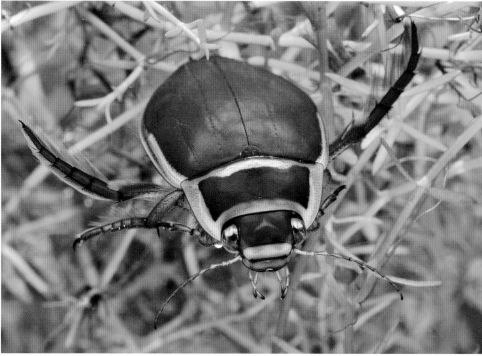

I've seen a lot of changes in the riverside I've known since childhood and I've come to realise that watching one area over a long period puts you in an ideal position to notice the small incremental changes that occur in the natural world.

I first saw this banded demoiselle damselfly early one evening. I knew right away that it was something new to the area – it was distinctive in flight because of the dark bands on the wings, and so different from the other dragonflies and damselflies that I see on the river. I stayed watching it, waiting until the evening air cooled and it was less capable of moving, so easier to photograph. This is one of the species that, possibly due to climate change, have gradually extended their range northwards in recent years.

Nature photographers create an archive of the natural world at a particular time, in a particular place, and so we are documenting changes that occur. I feel it's a responsibility of nature photographers to record these changes and use our images to attract the attention of a wider audience.

This great diving beetle takes me back to childhood days, visiting local ponds with jam jars in the hope of discovering something really exciting. At three centimetres in length, these beetles were always a prized find.

Searching for aquatic life in rivers was different again and I still remember finding a stone loach when I was a small boy – seeing a curious-looking fish beneath a rock and working out what it was, using my *Observer's Guide to Freshwater Fish*. Looking beneath rocks underwater revealed a whole other world; I always wondered what else I'd find under the next rock. This was easier in the river than in ponds – the fresh flowing water would imme-

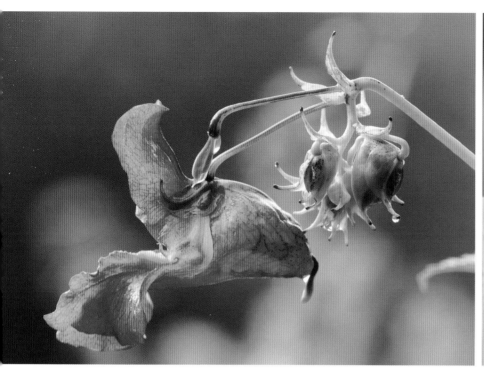
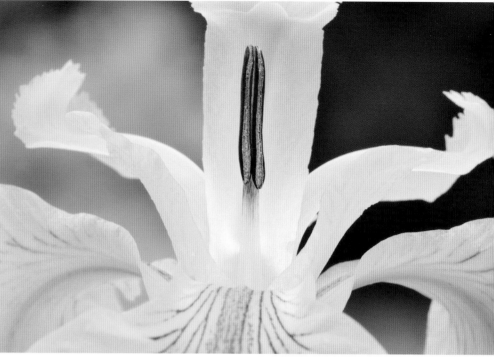

diately rinse away any cloudy silt that had been disturbed by moving the stones. For me, it was like panning for gold.

Now, I watch otters pouncing through the water and rummaging around on the riverbed, turning over rocks to dislodge the small fish sheltering beneath.

Himalayan balsam (*Impatiens glandulifera*) is widespread along the Tweed and considered a major weed – it spreads rapidly, as the seeds are carried along the river, and it shades out other vegetation. But it can be too easy to categorise plants as 'goodies and baddies'. There is

an upside: they are rich in nectar and flower late into the summer, the tall stands formed are a good place to see hoverflies and honey bees, and they provide cover for wildlife.

The sight of a yellow flag iris (*Iris pseudacorus*) takes me back to a favourite childhood haunt – a vibrant water meadow beside the Tweed, full of these bright flowers in early summer, where I'd spend hours exploring. It was all destroyed when the Berwick bypass was built. They're also evocative of the Outer Hebrides, where great swathes of them flourish in wet meadows and the upper shore. The dense

beds of their blade-like leaves form great cover for corncrakes. Here in the Borders they're not so plentiful but you still find them on wetlands. I spent three summer hours utterly absorbed in photographing this one flower head, experimenting with different lens setting to alter focus and exploring its lovely sculptural shapes from every angle.

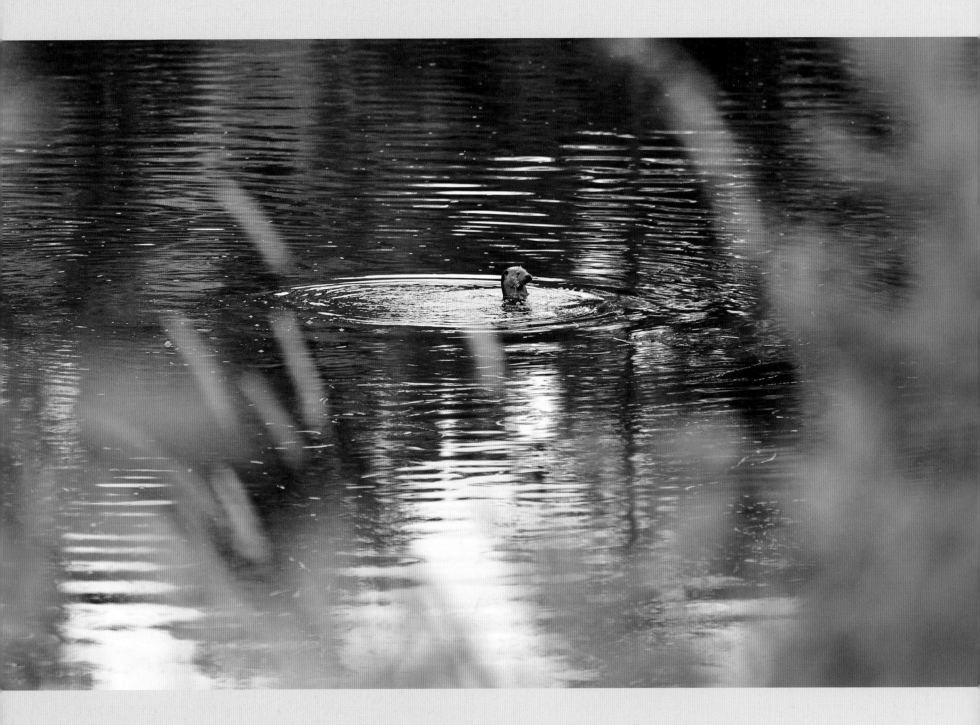

Glimpse

It's 6.30 a.m. and we're up on the bridge, gazing down at the great sweep of the river below. I peer through my binoculars at details such as ducks and ripples and edges. Laurie crosses to the other side, stops suddenly, checks through his binoculars: 'Got one!' he says triumphantly.

I dash across the bridge but can only see rock and river below. Laurie points and I lift my binoculars, hardly daring to hope, but there it is ... some distance away, tucked in against a small rocky cliff by the river-bank ... a brown head, then a splash. An otter! Then again, a brown head and a splash. It's porpoising, diving over and again in the same spot.

We hurry across the bridge and down the verge at the side of the road, scrambling over the crash barrier to peer at the river below. The otter is lying in the water, a long brown back and long dark tail stretched out on the surface like a dog on a rug. It looks straight up at us and holds our gaze for a moment. Then returns to its pouncing and diving, twisting its body and sliding into the water with a flourish of its elegant, tapered tail.

Sunbeams are playing in the river, brightening the rocks and making amber-coloured pools of light on the riverbed. There's a glimpse, a gleam of gold as the otter sleeks through one and the sunlight catches its coat. We wait and watch and hope, camera poised, but we don't see it surface. It's vanished.

We make our way down to the river, where we can watch at water level from the shelter of the scrub on the rocky shore. We settle on a small, island-like spit, with a perfect angle over the cliff wall and the river tumbling over the rocks.

Laurie sets me the task of keeping my binoculars trained on the gaps in the rocks, looking for a wee whiskery face peeping out. Then he sets to work constructing a small stone wall as a makeshift hide, something to shelter behind in future visits to this vantage point. He works deliberately, selecting the stones, weighing them in his hands, placing them together with a calm expertise. For a moment, he's both a man on a mission and a boy on the beach.

It's 8.30 already and I'm aware of the noise of the day – cars zooming past, dogs barking – joining the constant voice of the chattering river. It's OK to talk here, says Laurie, there's plenty of noise and the otters are accustomed to it. A handsome male goosander is lifted and rocked by the busy water, revealing its shining white belly as it is bounced down the rapids on a small weir. I'm scanning the gaps in the rocks, but there's still no sign of an ottery face.

We make for the angler's car park, where the motorhome and kettle are waiting. But, on the way, we take a detour to check out the opposite riverbank. The patterns of light and shade and the wind direction determine which bank Laurie chooses to explore, but he has a hunch that the otter is living nearby – he's often seen one here at dawn or dusk, slipping in and out of the woody debris. Ducking under branches and stepping over fallen trees, we explore the shingle shore.

'There!' says Laurie, as if we've found hidden treasure. At the water's edge, near a tangle of drift-wood and branches, there is a large mound of spraint on a rock, the moss burnt yellow all around it. This is more exciting to Laurie than a fleeting glimpse of an otter itself – spraint on this scale is not an otter passing by but a 'latrine' or otter toilet. It means the holt is close.

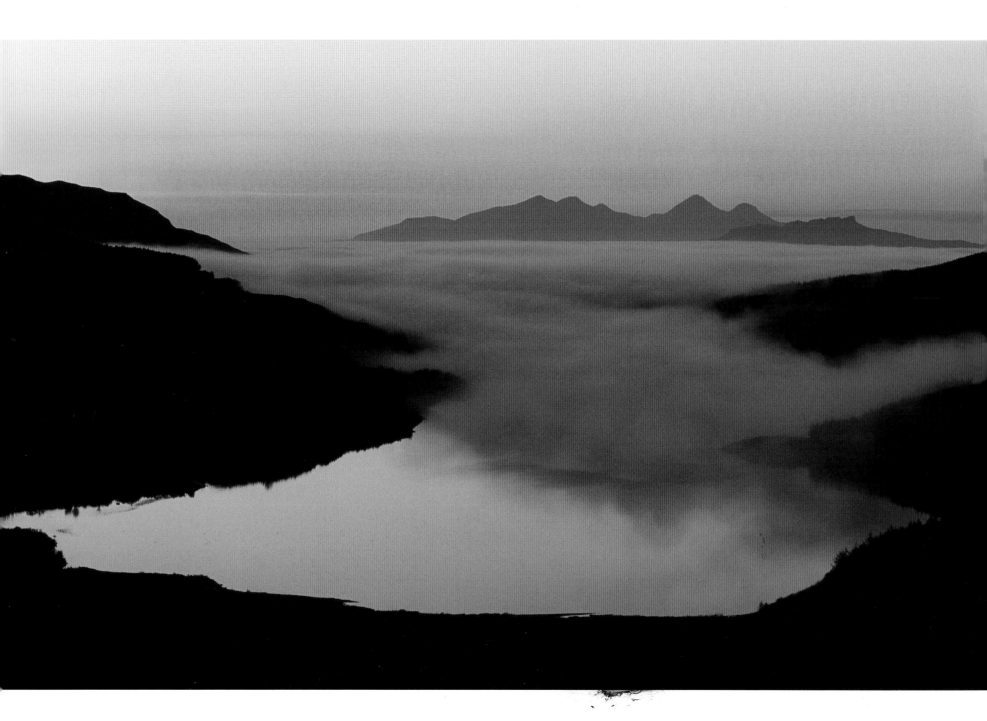

Chapter 4 Otters on the Western Shores

In the early 1980s, Laurie established both a business and a genre, becoming Scotland's first full-time professional nature photographer. He ploughed his own furrow many years before advances in digital technology helped to make nature photography both the international industry and popular pastime that it is today. As his pictures appeared in a range of magazines and publications, greetings cards and calendars, he quickly gained recognition for his own distinctive style. The photography built on his depth of understanding as a naturalist, showing wildlife in its context, animals at ease in their natural habitat; each picture a celebration of the beauty of natural light.

From his Berwickshire home, Laurie would head off for month-long field trips to remote locations in the Highlands and Islands, initially in a Morris Minor with a small tent from Woolworths, later in the relative luxury of a motor-

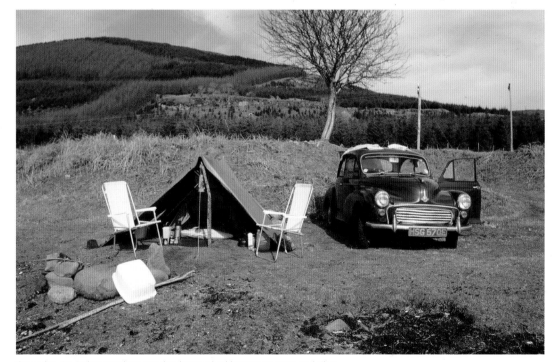

Opposite. An Ardnamurchan evening in May, looking out to Rum and Eigg.

Above. An early otter trip back in the early 1980s – wild camping on the shores of Mull's Loch Scridain.

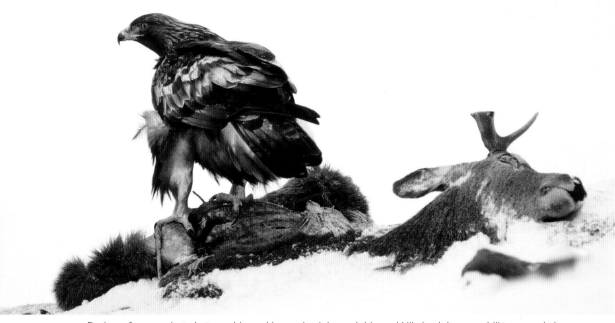

During a 6-year project photographing golden eagles, I dragged this road-killed red deer up a hill to use as bait.

home. His working life soon fell into a pattern that he calls 'commuting' – alternating between stints of work in his home beat and long trips to the north and west – that would continue for the next thirty years.

Laurie has always preferred to work under his own steam, exploring at his own pace and steadily building up a picture library with as comprehensive coverage as possible of Scotland's natural world. Some trips would target a particular species or habitat, but he'd always be happily distracted by whatever else intrigued him along the way. While lugging a dead deer up a mountain to bait golden eagles, for example, he came up with the idea of placing his camera in a fish tank in a mountain stream to capture the spectacle of spawning salmon that he had noticed in the same glen. While working on oystercatchers on the seashore, he took the time to photograph the intricate patterns of lichen on the rocks. Each piece of the jigsaw is equally relevant when your aim is to see the whole picture. By systematically returning to a range of habitats throughout Scotland, he has gathered more pieces and tried to improve on those he had, looking for greater detail or other aspects of behaviour, always searching for a new way to see a subject.

Otters were an appealing subject matter from the early days of Laurie's work. He has always found it an irresistible challenge to work on something that has rarely been photographed before and there were very few pictures of wild otters available at that time: most images that adorned calendars or greetings cards had been taken in wildlife parks or other captive situations.

In setting out to photograph otters in the wild, the obvious first step was to return to the scene of his first otter sightings from childhood holidays to the Ardnamurchan peninsula. Away from the main tourist routes through the Highlands, Ardnamurchan retains a feeling of wild remoteness, a sense of virgin territory. You have to walk to explore its isolated sandy bays and miles of windswept, rocky coastline. It's ideal otter territory, but makes for tricky terrain for photography. With no roads reaching much of the northern shore, exploration involved scrambling with heavy camera equipment over miles of rocky or boggy terrain and through dense rhododendron scrub. He had to cover a lot of ground in search of otters and then to move fast to keep up with them. But in time his perseverance paid off and he was rewarded with his first photographs of wild otters.

Laurie returned many times to Ardnamurchan, sometimes bringing his young family, and he managed to find and photograph otters on

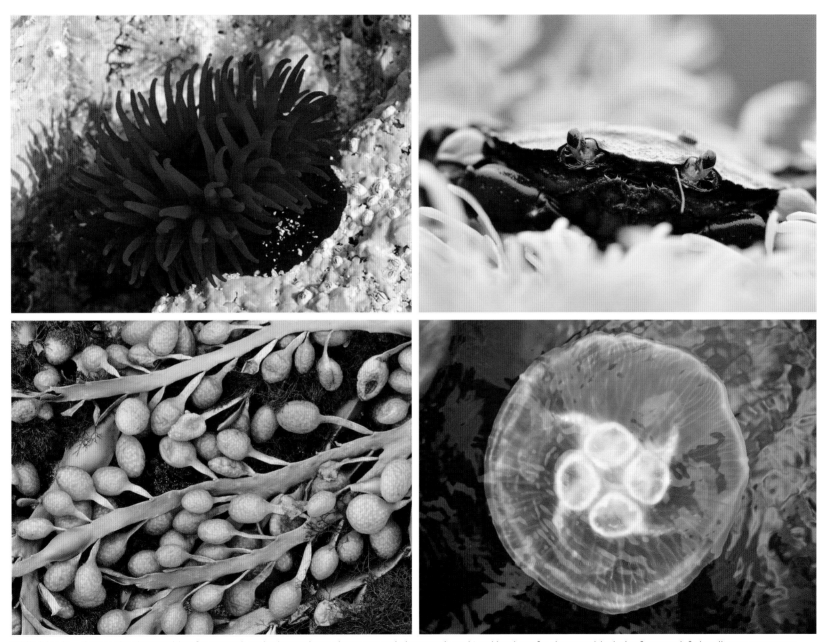

While lying low close to the shore waiting for otters there is always plenty else to see and photograph, and I go kitted out for close ups (clockwise from top left: beadlet sea anemone; shore crab; moon jellyfish and egg wrack sea weed). Sometimes I'm engrossed in photographing such details when an otter comes along . . .

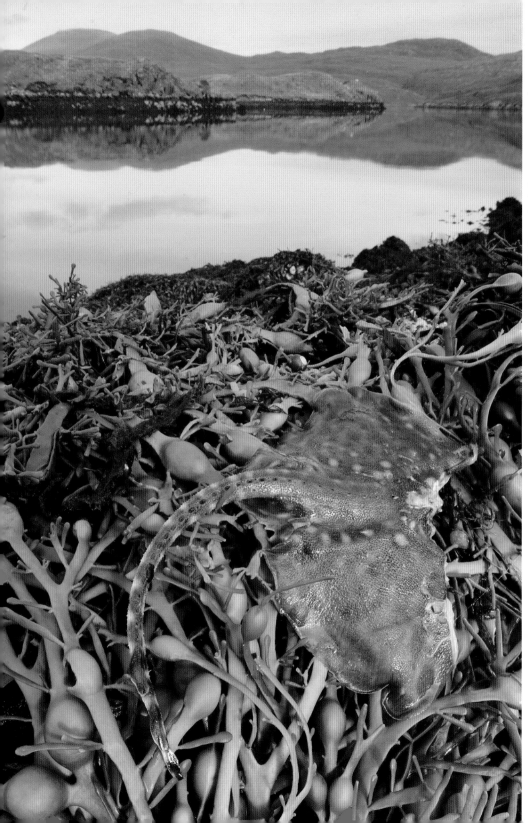

Left. I discovered this thornback ray which an otter had caught and eaten the head.

Opposite. I was lying on the shore under camouflage netting when this otter came to check me out under its own camouflage – by surfacing underneath the seaweed.

every trip. Through hours of patient observation, Laurie developed his radar for spotting otters on the shore. He learnt to work with the rhythm of the tides, and to go looking for them when the tide was falling or rising and the rocks and kelp beds were exposed. He learnt to spot their sleek forms in the sea or shore, to anticipate their movements and to read the wider landscape for signs of an otters' presence. Scanning a shoreline towards low tide, he could pick out the furry ball of an otter curled up like a cat, fast asleep on the seaweed-draped rocks.

In 1984, the wildlife film-maker Hugh Miles launched his seminal film and book *The Track of the Wild Otter*, the result of three years of filming otters on the shores of the Shetland Islands. When Miles embarked on the project, to film wild otters was considered 'an impossible task', but he eventually achieved it by getting out early, scouring the coast for days on end in all weathers, and working on a mixture of hunches, acts of faith and skilful observations. Laurie bought the book as soon as it came out and read it by paraffin lamp in his tent while camping in Ardnamurchan one winter. He found himself smiling and nodding as he read; Miles's vivid descriptions of the otters' lives resonated with his own experiences.

The skills honed in Ardnamurchan gave Laurie an intuitive feel for the right habitat, time of day and state of tide to find otters. He found this could be applied to any sea loch on Scotland's western seaboard, wherever his work

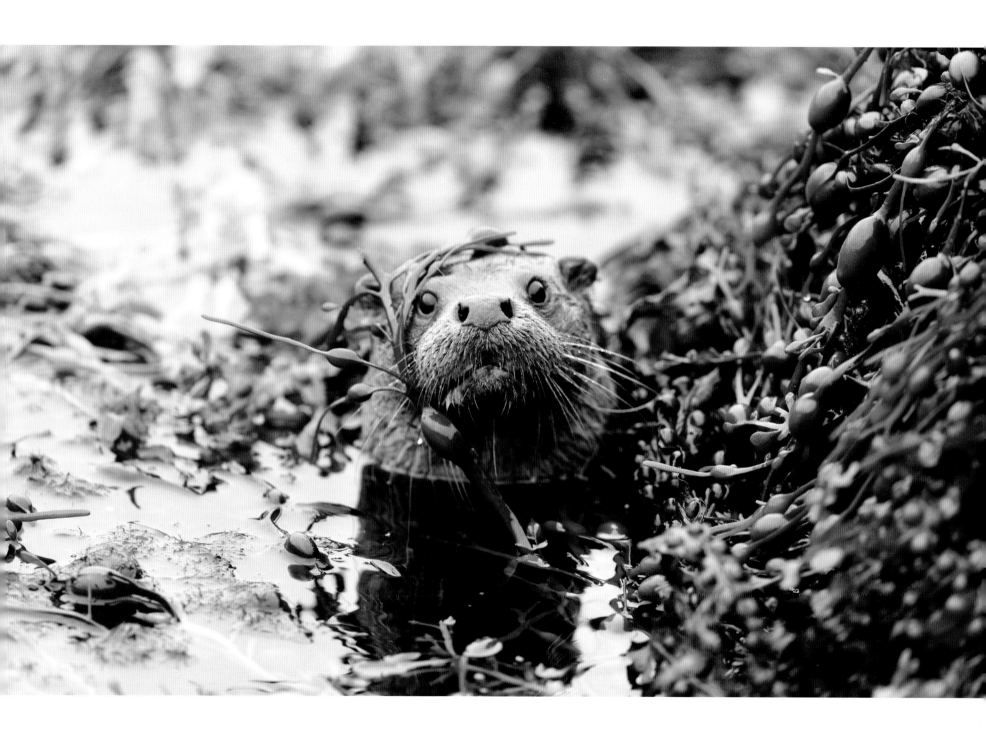

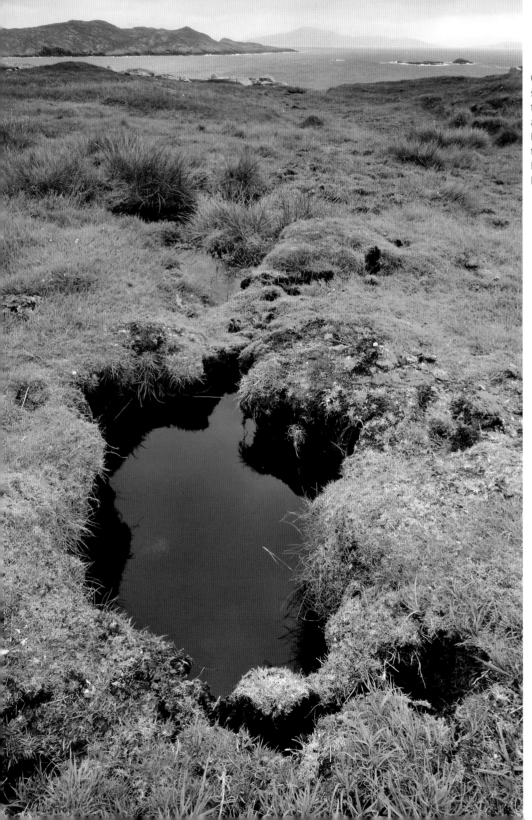

Otters that live in the sea still need access to freshwater – such as these pools on Harris. Without it their fur would become matted and lose its insulation.

took him. In the mid-1980s, for example, he made a series of long trips to the Outer Hebrides to photograph the landscape, flora and breeding birds of the machair – the flower-rich grassland that fringes the white sand beaches of the islands' western coast. Waders were present in vast numbers at that time and Laurie spent time photographing them against the exquisite backdrop of the Hebridean coast, adding species such as common snipe, redshank, ringed plover and the elusive corncrake to his growing image library. But while the gleaming beaches may have borne the prints of passing otters, this expansive setting wasn't rich otter habitat. So he would also take time to explore the rocky inlets of the east coast, and – in this more rugged habitat of rock pools and tangles of seaweed – he would find otters.

While Laurie mostly followed his muse, occasionally his travels were directed by commissions. He photographed feral goats living high on the sea cliffs of the Isle of Rum for the American Museum of Natural History, and later returned to the island to capture the landscape and wildlife over the course of a year for Scottish Natural Heritage. More recently Laurie was commissioned by the North Harris Trust to photograph their estate, one of the largest community-owned lands in Scotland, throughout the changing seasons. He used these opportunities to enhance his collection of wild otter pictures. In between tracking red deer in Rum or watching a golden eagles' eyrie in Harris, he

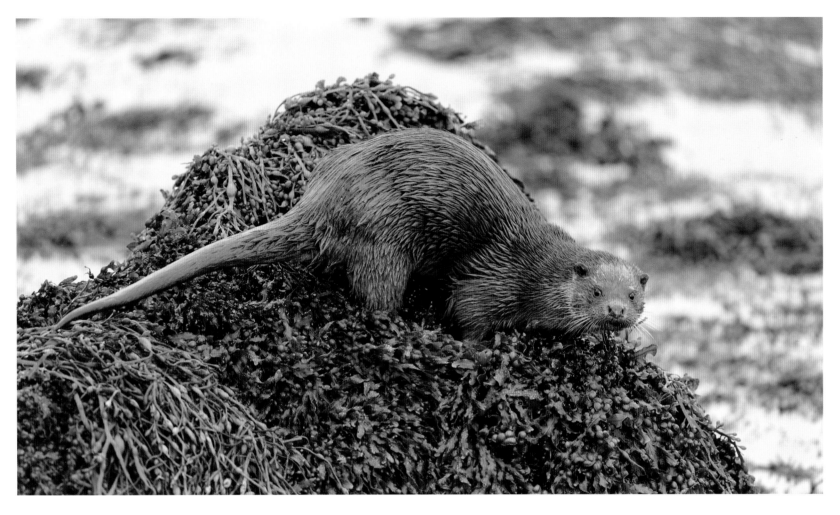

An otter sprainting in a prominent spot on the shores of Loch Maaruig in Harris.

would seek out otter habitat, and find them and photograph them – grooming, resting or play-fighting on the shore, peering out from under the kelp or up on a rock munching a lump-sucker fish.

These trips, from his home near the south-east coast of Scotland to the islands of the north and west, form the furthest reach of Laurie's regular 'commuting'. For him, that's far enough, as the country in between holds a staggering diversity of habitat types, more than enough to keep a nature photographer busy for the rest of his life.

But there was one exception: an opportunity to accompany the film-maker Hugh Miles to the Chilean Andes in 1994 in search of

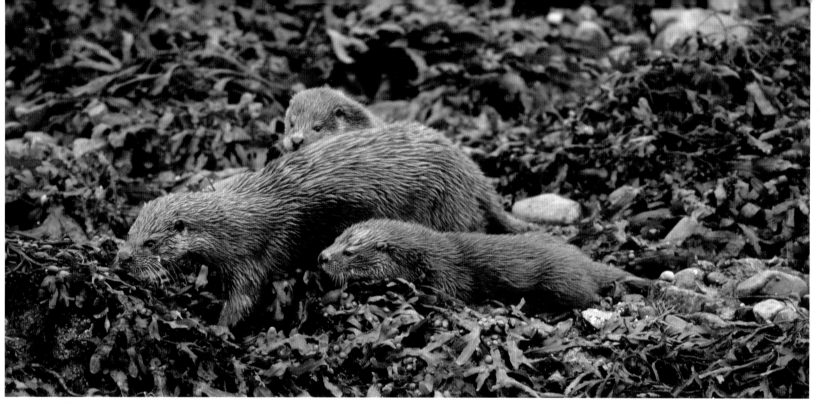

A mother and her cubs on the shores of Loch Linnhe in late September.

another elusive animal, the Patagonian puma. While filming the BBC's *Flight of the Condor* series (broadcast in the early 1980s), Hugh had discovered a population of pumas that had rarely been seen, let alone filmed. Realising that photographs would be needed to promote the new film, National Geographic television commissioned Laurie to join Miles. Laurie spent two months in Chile, eventually managing to photograph these almost mythical animals. He simply put in the time waiting beside a den until one animal became habituated to his presence and he could follow it as it left for a night's hunting in its mountain home.

The resulting photographs made a big impact.

Laurie has often been asked since whether the trip had whetted his appetite for more exotic travel, and why he has never joined the growing band of jet-setting wildlife photographers zooming around the world's biodiversity hotspots. He answers that although he enjoyed the trip immensely, he likes working his home beat just as much. It was exciting to search for pumas in the Andes and an exhilarating triumph to finally capture them on film. But it was equally exciting to spend nights in a hide in a snowy river valley near his home one deep winter, waiting for a woodcock to emerge, and

to satisfy a long-held ambition to achieve rare images of these secretive birds going about their daily lives. In the end, he says, it comes down to what you're happiest doing. For Laurie, it's not about what subject he is photographing or where, but the freedom to follow his muse, to capture his experience and tell his own story. And there's nowhere better to do that than the landscape he's known intimately all his life.

Shortly after he returned from Chile, Laurie's second son was born. With a growing family and a growing image library to find space for, it was time to move house. As a successful nature photographer, he could have lived

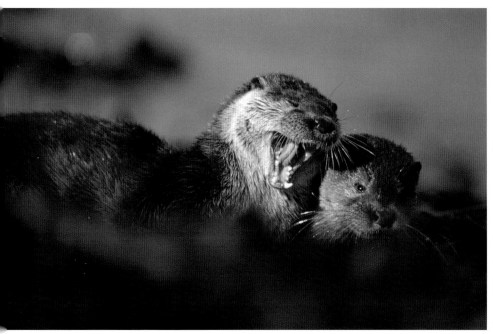

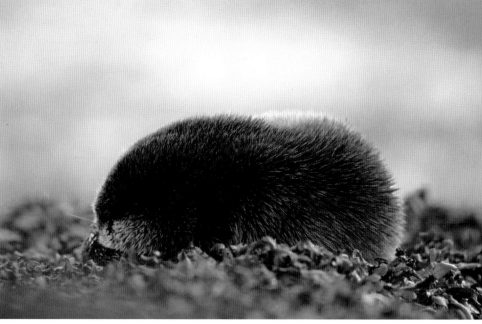

Winter afternoon sunlight on the shores of Loch Don in Mull, these two otters were draped over each other during a lull between the tides.

After watching for an hour, I just crept away from this sleeping otter. It never knew I had been there.

anywhere in Scotland, and considered moving north to the Highlands, with the appealing prospect of a wilder landscape and species such as pine martens and golden eagles on his home beat. But after much deliberation the family moved 50 yards, to a larger house in the same village. There's enough here, he decided, and still so much to explore and discover. There was pioneering work to be done in photography, not by travelling further but by looking ever closer.

So in between trips throughout Scotland, and very occasional forays abroad (often to lecture on the benefits of working close to home), Laurie continues to work mostly on his home turf. He studied the long golden stretches of dune-backed beaches where he'd collected common lizards as a child, the rivers where he'd watched the grey herons, mute swans and kingfishers, and the woodlands with their badgers, bats and tawny owls. He focused even closer on the birds, plants and pondlife in his own garden – realising you don't have to go anywhere to achieve the aim of seeing things in a new way.

Watching a habitat so intensely over a period of time means you're well placed to notice changes in the natural world. Nature photographers are inadvertently documenting these changes, recording the impact of climate change as some species creep north; of intensive farming practices as others decline; or sometimes of the benefits of conservation efforts as species recover. Over the course of Laurie's work he's noticed how the water voles and cuckoos have largely disappeared from the region, while buzzards, once unknown, are now an everyday sight. He has been able to document new species reaching Scotland from the south, such as comma butterflies and nuthatches. And then he began to hear rumours, and barely dared to believe that they were true – were there otters on the Tweed again?

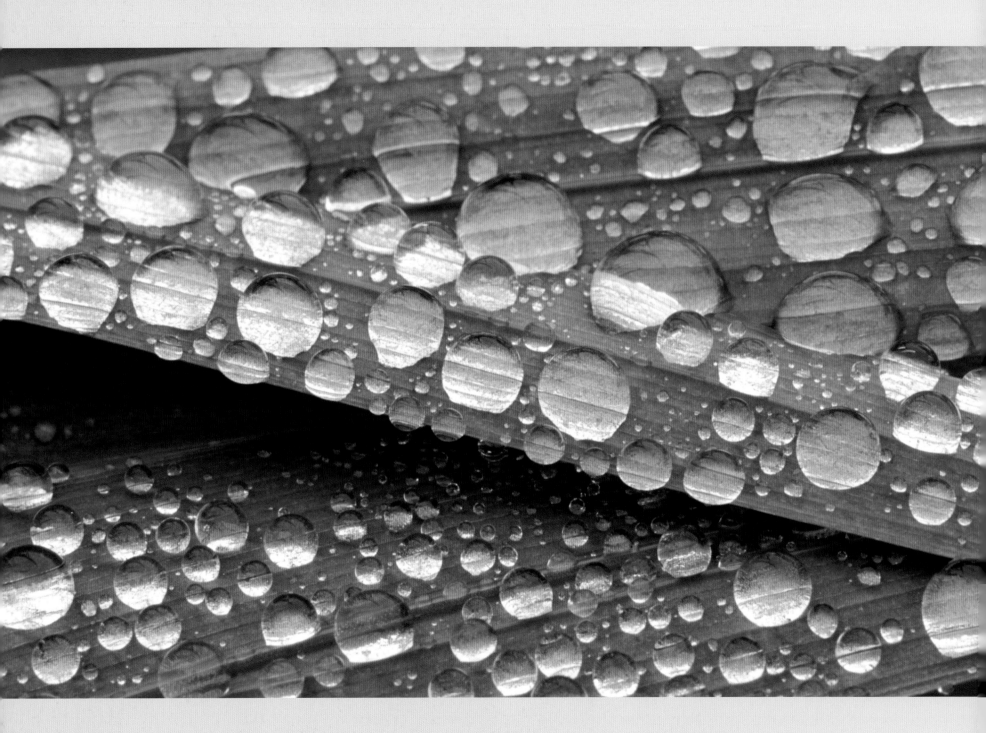

Rain

There's a smudge of silver on the wooden path beside the water. Just a gleam on the wet boards. Laurie stops and crouches down to examine it, like a hunter on a trail.

Fish scales, he says softly, explaining, almost in a whisper, that otters will devour small prey in the water but need to land a big fish to eat it. So any fishy remains suggest an otter's recent presence.

We walk on, following the wide curves of the Tweed along the riverside path, scanning the water and the banks for signs of otters. I notice yet again that Laurie sees more than the rest of us. Even when he's not holding a camera to his eye, he's looking at the world through a wide-angle lens, then homing in on the smallest detail. He takes in the whole span of the river at a glance, yet notices the dew on a spider's web. He points out a tunnel of flattened vegetation where otters have made their way along the riverside, and the nicks in the bank where they slip in and out of the water, and the heron on the opposite bank that takes off, lifting its bulk into the air with improbable grace.

The river is big and swollen, a wide expanse of rolling, surging, brown water. And we're looking in it for a small brown head about the size of an orange. Laurie says how hard it is to see them, that 'getting your eye in' is everything. Look for something that goes against the grain, he says, something different, like a movement or a sudden splash.

I'm looking. There is movement everywhere and sudden splashes all over the place. The river is taunting me, dancing over rocks that could be an otter's head, flicking up sticks that could be the tapered tip of an otter's tail.

Great big splashes of raindrops start to fall, leaving pockmarks on the water's surface. We take refuge in one of the fisherman's huts along the riverside and stand in silence at the entrance, watching the rain and the river outside.

I'm mesmerised by the body of water rushing past, the way it moves, throwing words around my head in an attempt to find one worthy of describing it. It strikes me that one of the reasons otters are so difficult to spot is that they're so like the river itself. Each word I try fits otters, too: powerful, playful, muscular, twisting, turning, flowing, surging, splashing, rippling . . . as if otters are river incarnate.

There's a harsh 'krar krar' from the opposite bank. 'Did you hear that jay?' asks Laurie.

The rain is getting heavier. It's nearly 9 a.m. now, late in otter terms – they're likely to have fed and played and looped and curled and headed back to their holts by now. Slowly we make our way back along the wet riverbank, still willing the rolling water to yield up an otter.

It doesn't. Yet I'm feeling strangely elated, despite the rain and the longing for a cup of tea. I'm remembering that lovely Alice Walker title, *Horses Make a Landscape Look More Beautiful*. It's true. I work from an attic office and from my desk I can see a few distant fields over the rooftops. A tiny silhouette of a horse in the corner of a field lifts the whole view. And otters . . . they make the landscape more exhilarating. I can see the paths myself now, otter-width, flattened grass by the water's edge, closer to the river than our path. The riverbank feels alive, tingling with the promise of their presence.

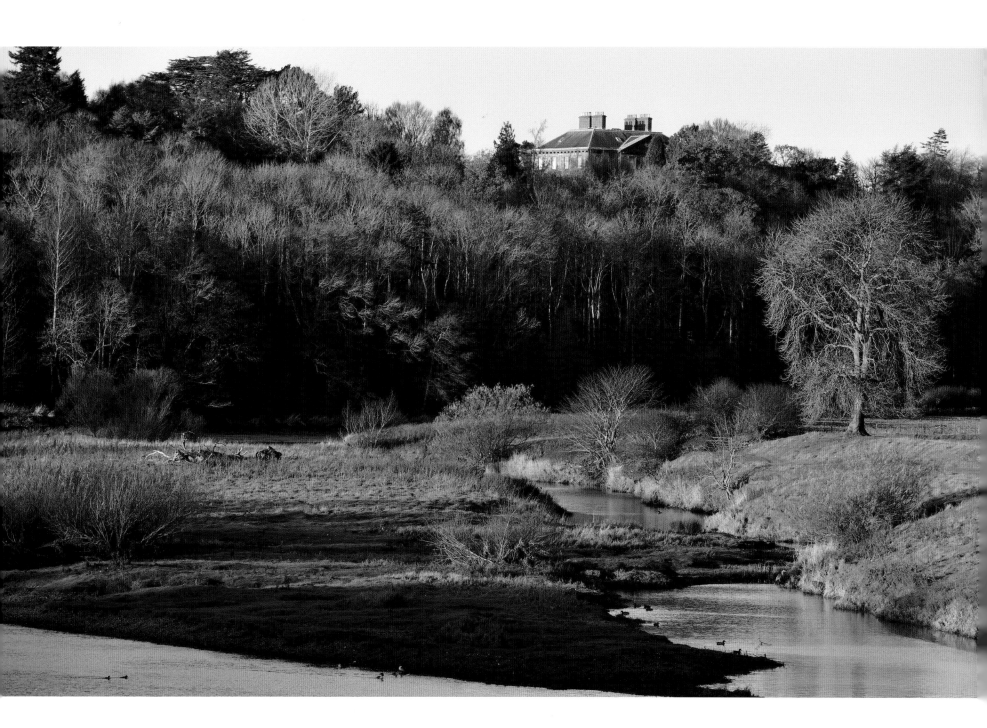

Chapter 5 Autumn

There's almost an in-between season before autumn really happens: a quiet, damp, muddy limbo when the birds are looking tatty and the plant life is dying away. The riverbanks are scented with a sweet mustiness from the decaying leaves of the butterbur. It's easier to see wildlife on the river now, as the riotous summer growth is reduced to yellowing grasses, nettles and the last of the Himalayan balsam stands – trace your hands over their spring-loaded seed pods and they snap and leap with surprising velocity.

Then the temperature drops and everything lifts; there's a cool, clear, crispness in the air and the bank-side trees begin to blaze. It's a season of migrant birds returning, of dew hanging like jewels in spiders' webs and swirls of mist drifting over the morning river. This is also the main season for salmon. The autumn rains trigger salmon runs that draw people from all over the world in pursuit of this 'king of fish'.

Though the days are getting shorter, the light is more usable for photography throughout the day, without the overhead glare of summer. With the sun low in the sky, the softer, oblique light adds greater depth, texture and richness of colour to the landscape.

This was taken from the Chain Bridge, or Union Bridge as it's officially known, which spans the River Tweed, linking England and Scotland. When it opened in 1820 it was the longest wrought iron suspension bridge in the world that could carry vehicular traffic. It's also the perfect vantage point to watch, undetected, over the wild world of the river below.

I've spent many hours working here over the years, watching as the day turns to dusk and nocturnal wildlife comes to life along the river, or in the early mornings when the 'day shift' takes over. On this still morning in late autumn, the golden light was boosting the last of the late autumn colour, highlighting what little colour is left in the woods surrounding Paxton House that stands on the skyline.

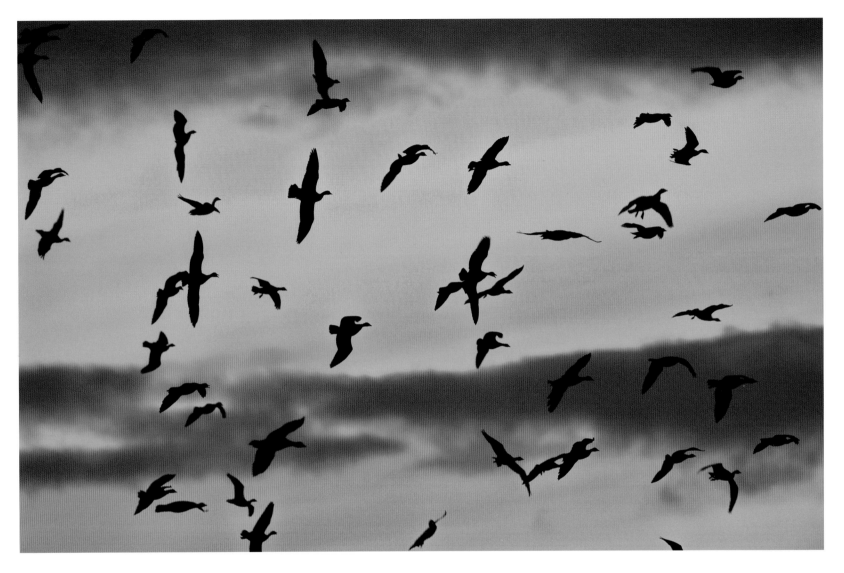

I make an annual pilgrimage to a moor loch in the Lammermuir Hills to see the pink-footed geese arriving in their thousands at sunset. During the day, they feed on the stubble fields across the Merse, the low-lying fertile plain either side of the Tweed and between the Cheviot and Lammermuir hills, sometimes in mixed flocks with the mute swans. Towards evening they come in to the loch to roost, in the safety of the water. Here they are 'whiffling' – which is rather like 'falling with style': as they approach the water, they tip sideways and drop from the sky to hasten their descent.

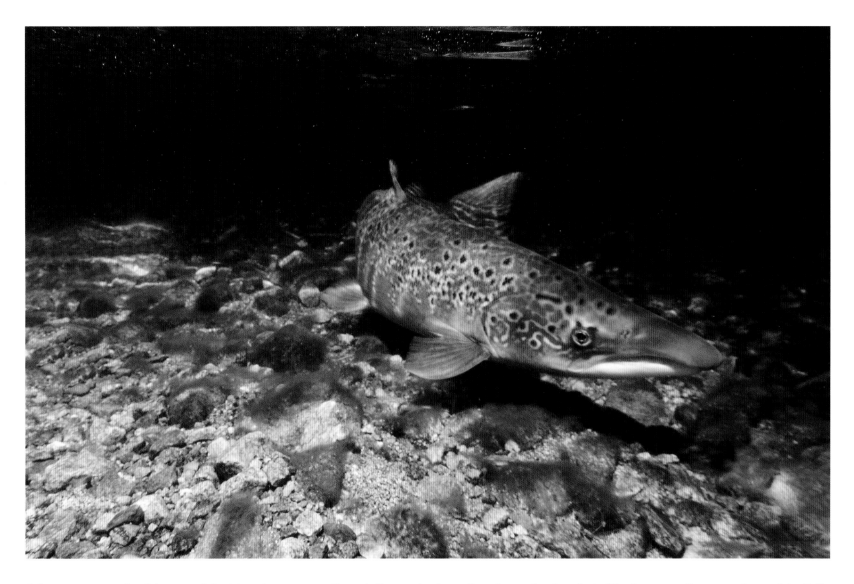

Salmon are central to life around the Tweed, to the wildlife in the river and to the local economy. It's said that each fish caught by the rods is worth several hundred pounds to the area in terms of tourism, hotels, restaurants and shops, as well as ghillies and others directly involved with angling. Everything revolves around the salmon here and their healthy numbers at present are a testament to a clean river.

Otters will go after salmon at every stage in their life, from small parr to huge fish. Fully grown salmon are capable of getting away from an otter and I've seen some writhing, slippery fights between them!

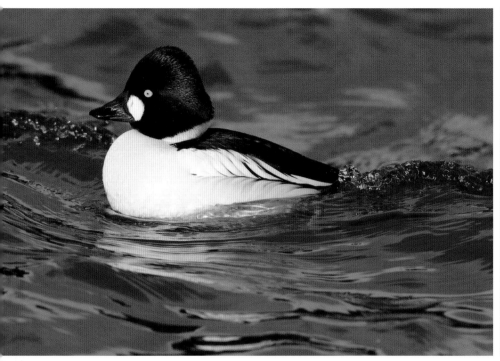

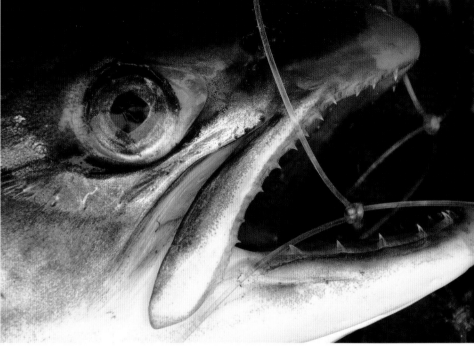

The River Tweed is a nationally important site for goldeneye, hosting a significant over-wintering population of these neat, endearing little ducks. You see larger numbers in the lower reaches of the river and when they take off as a flock there's a whistling sound from their wing beats. They disperse through the winter along the river, but a hard core remain near the estuary.

The goldeneyes we see on the Tweed breed in the boreal forests of Scandinavia and over-winter here. There's an intrigue about migratory birds; I can only imagine what they've seen or had to contend with – maybe wolverines and bears? The stories they could tell . . .

There are also small populations now resident year round in the Scottish Highlands, attracted by specially designed nestboxes that are put up for them in trees close to water – sometimes I've found pine martens holed up in these boxes!

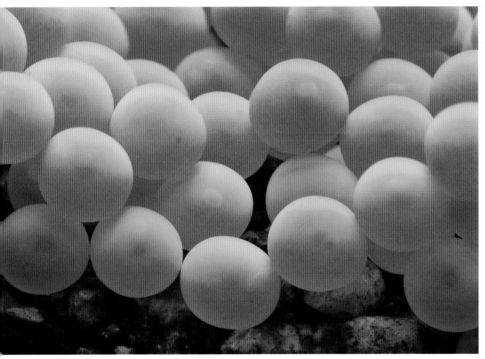 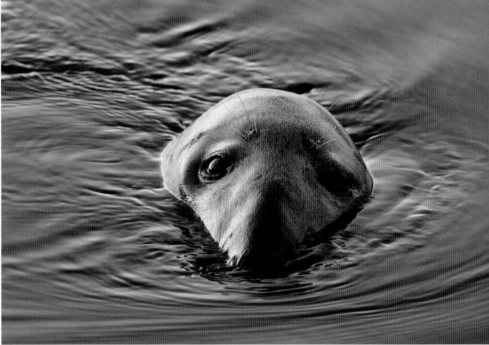

Poaching is a serious issue around here. It's no longer a question of an individual taking 'one for the pot', but big business. There is a sinister side to it, too, with violent clashes between poachers and bailiffs. Fine, monofilament nets are commonly used, occasionally entrapping and drowning otters and waterbirds alike.

Sometimes even poisonous chemicals are used, which affect everything else in the water as well.

This image of salmon eggs was taken in the gravelly areas high in the tributaries where the salmon were born and where they return to spawn.

In autumn I begin to see grey seals coming quite far up the river. The Tweed is tidal as far as Paxton House – already several miles upstream – and beyond, and the seals come in with the tide, feeding on the salmon, especially in the deeper pools.

I spotted this juvenile otter out foraging, working its way along the side of a river, parallel to the bank, so I was able to keep up with it and follow it for more than an hour. Occasional joggers and dog walkers would come along the path where I was working. Sometimes people see an otter and stand there pointing or holding their mobile phone up to photograph it! They often don't appreciate what a difference it would make if they crouched down to watch, still and silent. They would see so much more. So the otter would disappear when people came by, but not for long. It just retreated for a while and if I gave it a bit of time and could work out its direction of travel I could usually pick it up again.

The river was really clear this day and the otter was behaving like a goosander! I've often seen goosanders swimming along with their heads dipped in the water; they'll go for quite a distance like that. This otter wasn't diving – the water was quite shallow – it was just swimming along, looking underwater for prey.

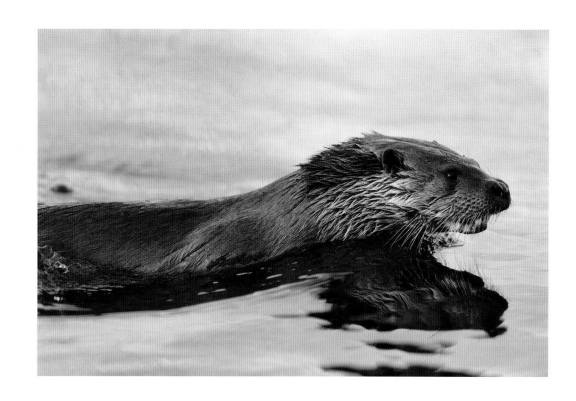

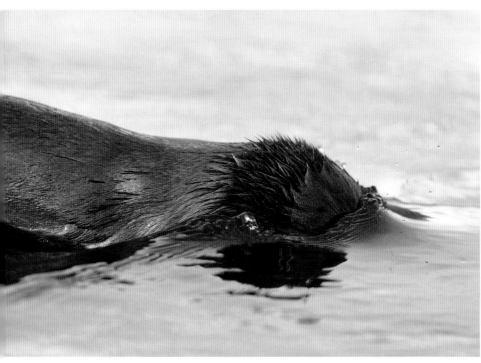 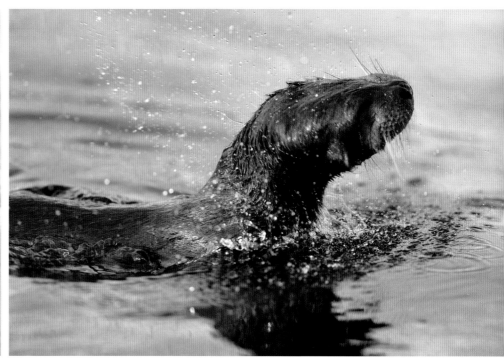

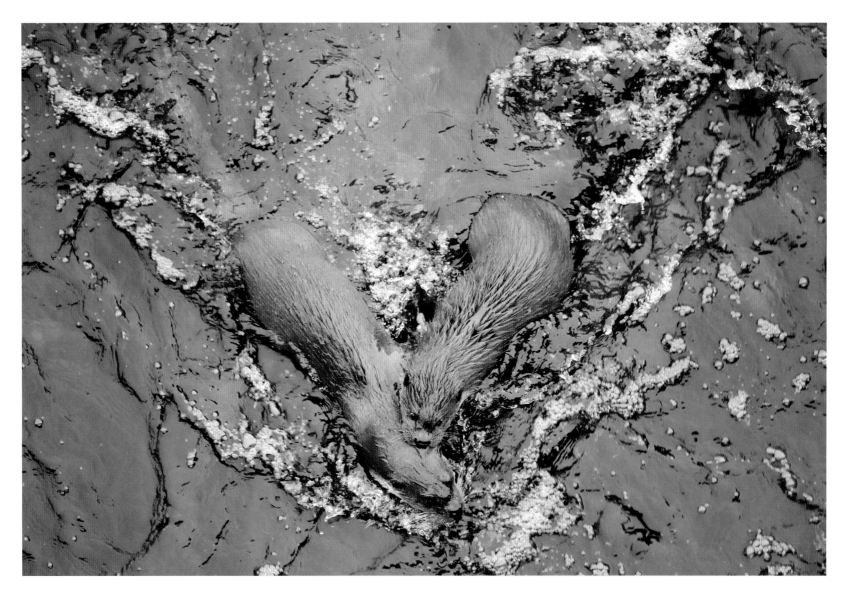

Adolescent otters will 'hang out' together before leaving to find territories of their own. I was familiar with this pair of juveniles and I knew that as dusk fell they would be heading upstream for a night's fishing. On this evening the prevailing wind precluded my normal position on the riverbank, so I settled for a vantage point on a bridge, well above their noses. Like many animals, otters rarely look up, so I could watch undetected for longer periods, enabling me to enjoy these siblings play-fighting directly beneath me.

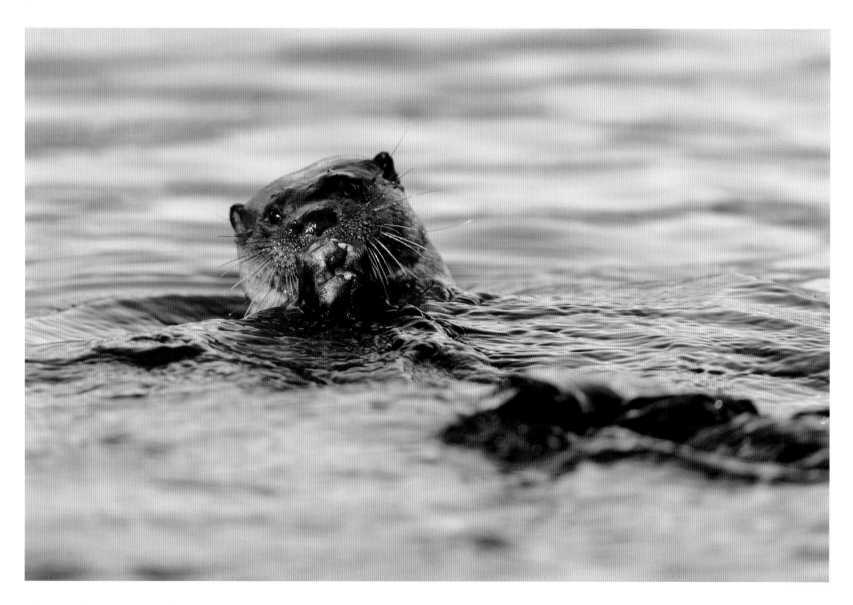

This was the same juvenile otter as pictured on page 84, and at one point it lay on its back, holding its prey in its front paws – a behaviour normally associated with the sea otters in the Californian kelp forests. I've rarely photographed this behaviour and I wondered what it was eating that it had to hold it in this way while it dealt with it.

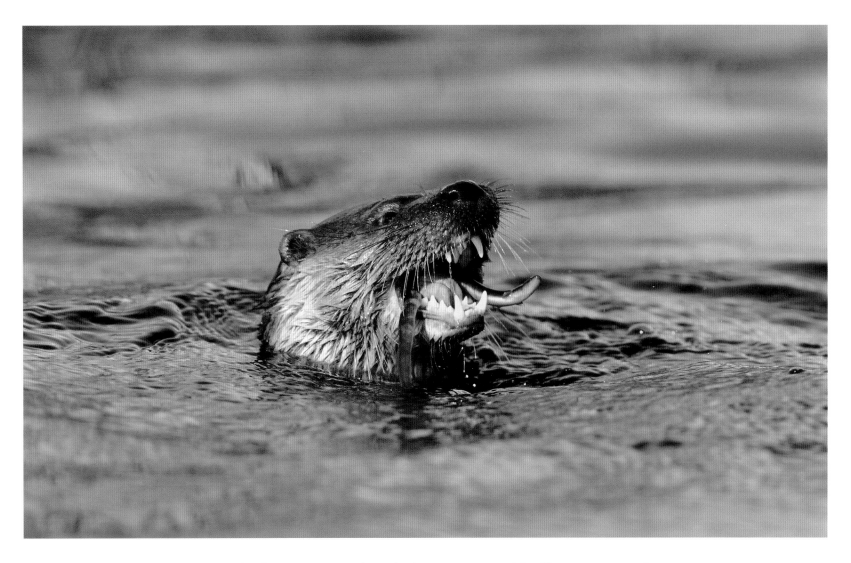

Revealing its impressive canine teeth, this young otter surfaced to chomp on a young eel. At this stage in their life cycle, eels are sometimes known as 'yellow eels' because of the colour of their underside. Like salmon, they come into the Tweed and make their way upstream through the river system. They'll negotiate whatever's in their way, such as rocks or waterfalls, even slithering over land, if necessary. But eels are in the river to feed not to spawn – European eels reproduce far across the Atlantic in the Sargasso Sea and drift across the ocean as tiny larvae.

Eels have declined drastically in recent years and their conservation status is listed as critically endangered.

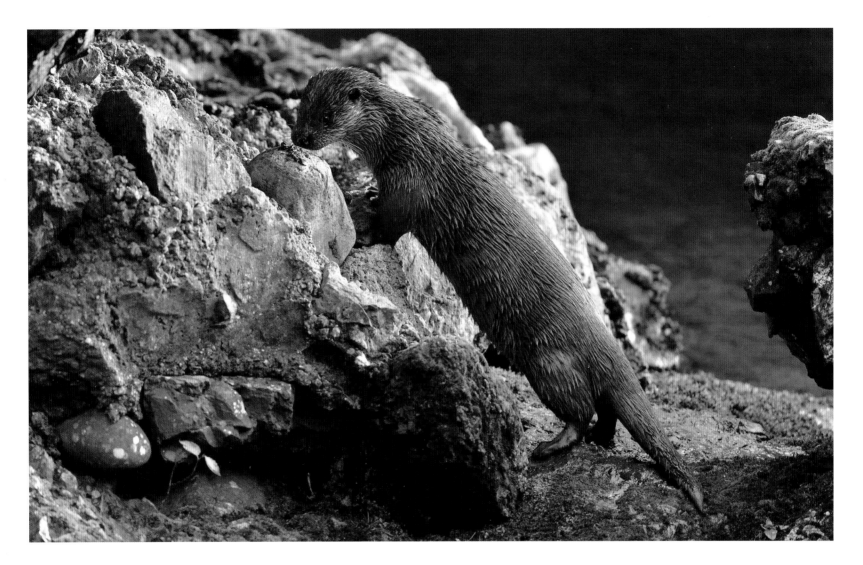

Otter spraint may look subtle to us, but to the otters themselves, spraint is an important signal to mark territory and to communicate information. They are very deliberate about where they leave their spraint, and spend quite some time investigating the scents of others. This otter was a regular at this site – a very good fishing ground and so an important territory. I watched it sniffing intently to see who else had been around – rather like dogs and lampposts!

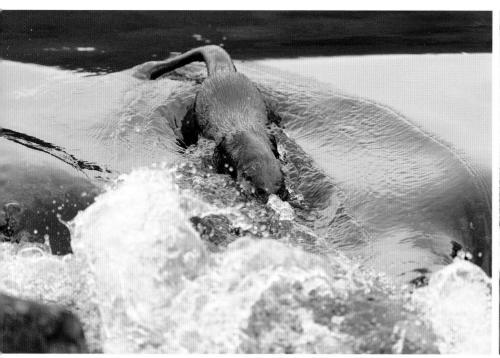 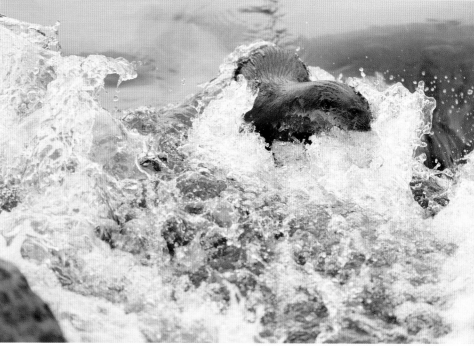

I'd been watching this otter fishing on the weir for some time and wanted to capture an image of it descending through the rushing water. It shows something of the otter's strength and ease: there was a pretty forceful current, yet the otter was able to go in and pause and rummage around. However, there was just a grazed grass field beside the weir, with no bank-side cover to hide behind or to disguise my silhouette, so it required some strategic planning. I identified the spot I wanted to work from in order to get close-ups of the otter in the weir and began to gather bits and pieces of woody debris from the river and build it up into a small pile there. Over the following days I watched from a distance to see how the otter would react. It noticed the pile immediately and would keep glancing at the suspicious new shape on the skyline. It took a couple of weeks until the otter accepted it, after which I developed a technique where I would run forward when the otter was underwater and throw myself down behind the heap and poke the camera lens over the top. It only worked this once – many other times I saw the otter but didn't have time to get myself into position and the otter would be over the weir in a flash. But this time something caused it to pause for just long enough and I got the series of pictures I wanted.

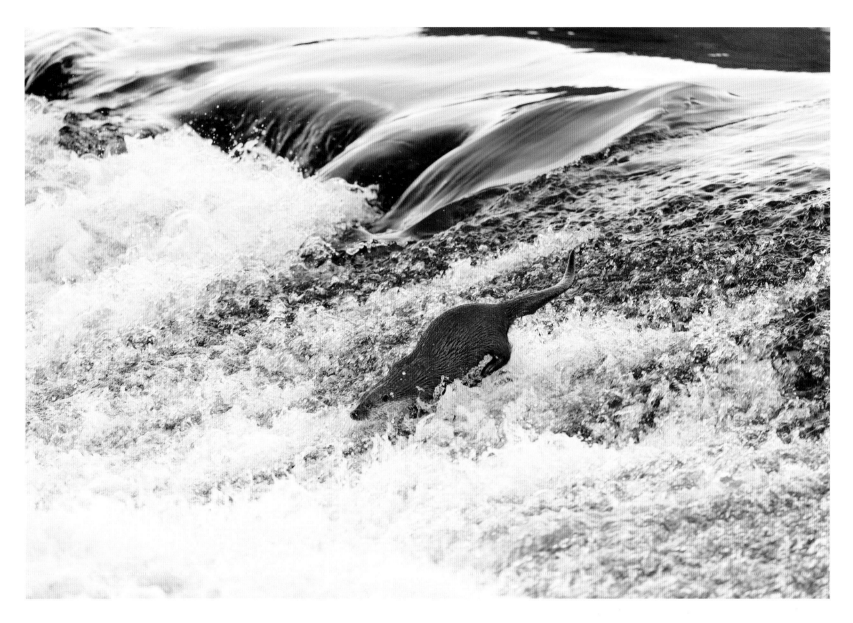

I discovered a favoured feeding site on a pool beneath a weir that had once powered one of the many oat mills on the Whiteadder, a tributary of the Tweed. I'd been in place behind a tree trunk since the very early morning when this otter made its way down the weir against the attractive backdrop of cascading water. I stayed and watched as it hunted, feeding on several trout before disappearing downstream.

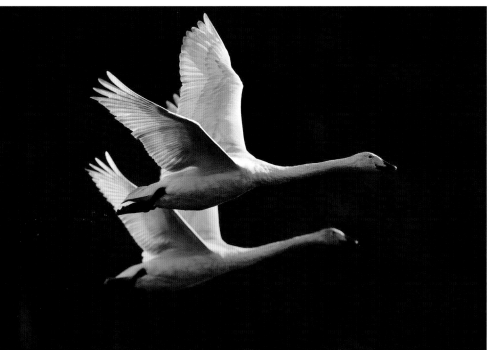 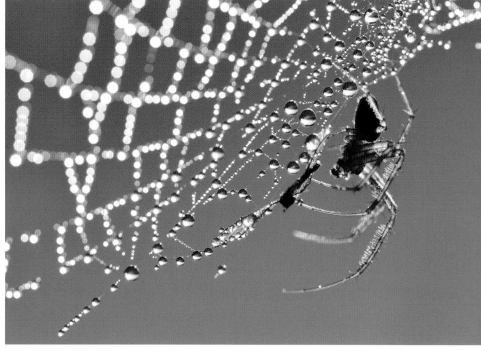

Like wintering geese, whooper swans spend their autumn and winter here, roosting at night on the quieter waters of the Tweed and its islands, and frequently staying in family groups. They feel safe from predators in such places, which is probably more of an issue in their northern homelands than here. These birds come from very wild areas of Iceland, northern Scandinavia and Russia. They are very wary compared to the Tweed's resident mute swans and can be as difficult as golden eagles to work with. They always seem to have one or two individuals on lookout while the rest are feeding or roosting. Watching through a telescope from two or three hundred yards away, I can tell by their body language when I'm too close – one false move and they're away.

On dewy mornings in autumn, the last of the riverside foliage looks like it is slung with tiny hammocks and bound in an intricate lace. There are more cobwebs around than we realise, it's just that we only see them when certain weather conditions reveal them. If I zoom in I can see the landscape in miniature in the tiny droplets.

Thousands of pink-footed geese congregate to roost on and around moorland lochs in the

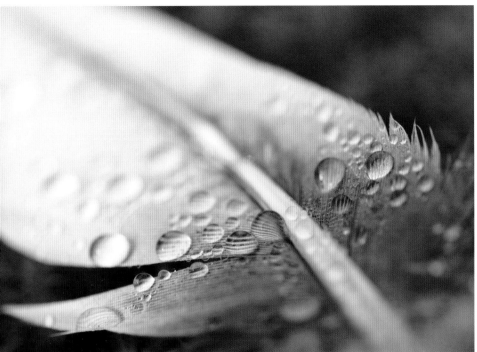
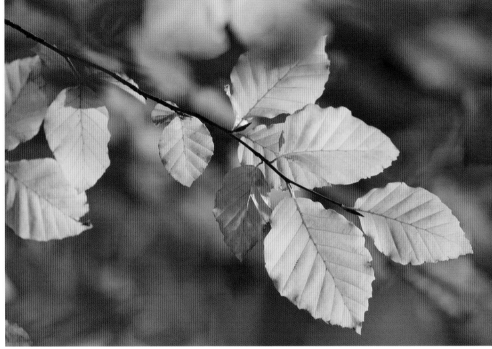

upper reaches of the river system and so a lot of preening goes on – leaving a 'litter' of feathers lying around in the grass. Again it's about stopping and looking at something that you could easily pass by without noticing – like the way there are pictures within pictures, each droplet of water acting as a magnifying glass, magnifying the filament of the feather.

The beech leaves at the water's edge made me stop and look closer – I was thinking about how the leaves will soon fall and drift into the river, swirling around on the surface and then sinking down, contributing their nutrients to the food chain, becoming part of the rich cycle of life that links every living thing on and around the river.

Fishermen

There is a path, and there are steps, that wind from the car park where we are down to the river where we're going otter-exploring this evening. But that wouldn't be Laurie's way of getting from A to B. You'd miss too much along the way.

So we step over the wooden barrier from the car park straight into the woods. As we do, two young badger cubs come bowling out of the trees, startle as they see us and bound away. We've stepped into badger city. Laurie points out the sett all around us, the mounds of compacted, almost polished earth. He's watched generations of badgers here, seen new entrances developing, seen badger families grow, work the earth, construct their homes and toilets, their routes through the woodland and down steep badger-smoothed slopes, shaping their landscape.

We stride downhill through a tangle of under-growth. There's a movement ahead and a badger starts and stiffens, upright at the entrance to its sett, nose in the air. Laurie's seen it already and is utterly still. We're all three frozen in position, staring at each other, like three creatures in Narnia turned to stone. I feel a five year old's urge to giggle in the silence, but also a profound peace. Through the trees I can see shafts of evening sunlight pouring out from under the clouds, flooding the horizon with a wash of gold.

There's a sharp mewing call from a buzzard circling above us.

'Must be a nest,' whispers Laurie.

I want to ask questions – what are the other bird calls, the bubbles of flutey sounds from the trees – but I don't want to intrude on the silence, or startle the badger, or end the staring competition we're engaged in.

Then there's a big crunch and a snap of twigs, loud sounds that feel almost comical in our silence. Paying no heed to our reverential hush, three badgers come bustling along behind us, a family outing in the woods. Very slowly we turn to the sound and they see us, pause for a startled moment, then scamper along in their bumbling way to their sett. Our badger seizes the moment and disappears from view. We remain still.

'It's still here,' says Laurie quietly. 'Just at the sett entrance.' But we leave it in peace and continue on through the woods, stepping past nettles, over wires and fences, out of the darkness of the trees and down to the surprisingly light expanse of evening river.

There are voices here. A group of fishermen working at low water, with two wooden boats and a lot of netting. The boats are known as cobbles; these are some of the last of an ancient fishing tradition that once engaged a thousand people on the Tweed. Some of the fishermen recognise Laurie and nod a greeting; we stop to chat and enquire about otter sightings.

George introduces himself. He wears a cap and has a smiling, leathery, tanned face. He tells me about the fishing, how you can see the salmon approaching around the curve of the river, the 'v's of their wake in the water, 'coming like wee speed boats'. He says he hasn't seen an otter for a month or so, but one was hanging around when he was building a new landing stage: 'a cheeky fellow playing chicken with the dogs'. The dogs would run into the water and the otter would disappear, then pop up again as soon as the dog was back on land, coming ever closer, as if teasing it. Confident when in the water, the otter wasn't both-ered by the men working, but it would remain in sight as they dug into the riverbank.

We leave the men to their boats and nets and the bright river. They're working together in silence, their hands making smooth, synchronised movements as they bring the nets in, until there are large, glistening salmon flapping and writhing and smacking their silver tails on the shore.

We walk along the shining river for a while, searching it with our eyes. The surface is utterly still – we'd spot the 'v' of an otter's wake a long way off

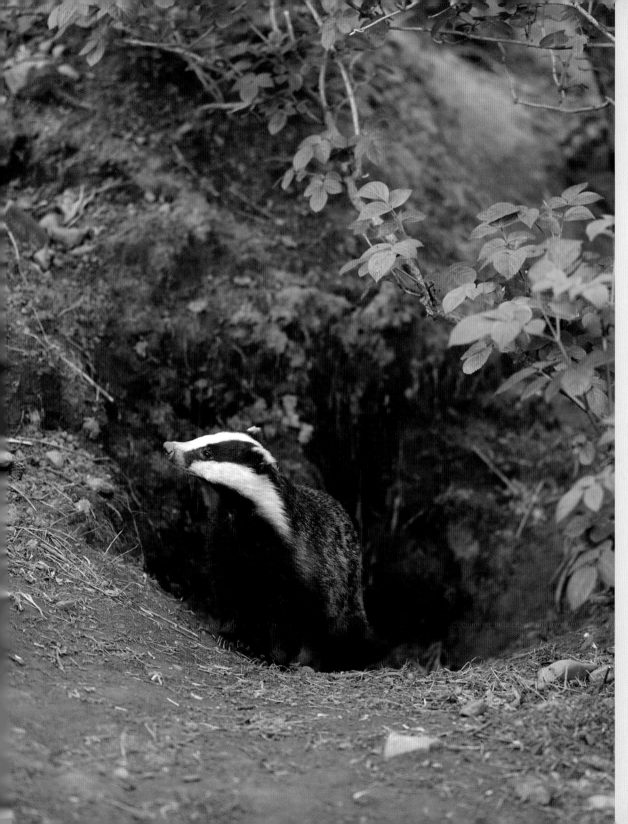

in these conditions, but there's no movement at all, just the polished gleam from the golden sky. It's darker in the woods now, as we weave a different route back to the car park, passing a pond, where something has parted the weed on the surface of the water. We find spraint here, but it's dusty and crumbly, not a fresh clue. Still we take a potted tour of otter memories and moments, revisiting the places where Laurie first saw otters here in the early days; the streams they use as culverts down to the river, where he'd catch a glimpse dashing into the shelter of thick undergrowth.

The sky has deepened from gold to indigo by the time we reach the car park. I don't want to break the spell of the evening by returning to cars and houses. But then we're back at Laurie's office, sitting around the computer, pouring over a feast of photos and there's a shuffle outside. Laurie has been habituating the local badgers, luring them closer with the promise of an evening snack. Through the glass door between his office and the garden, a long black-and-white face is looking in at us.

95

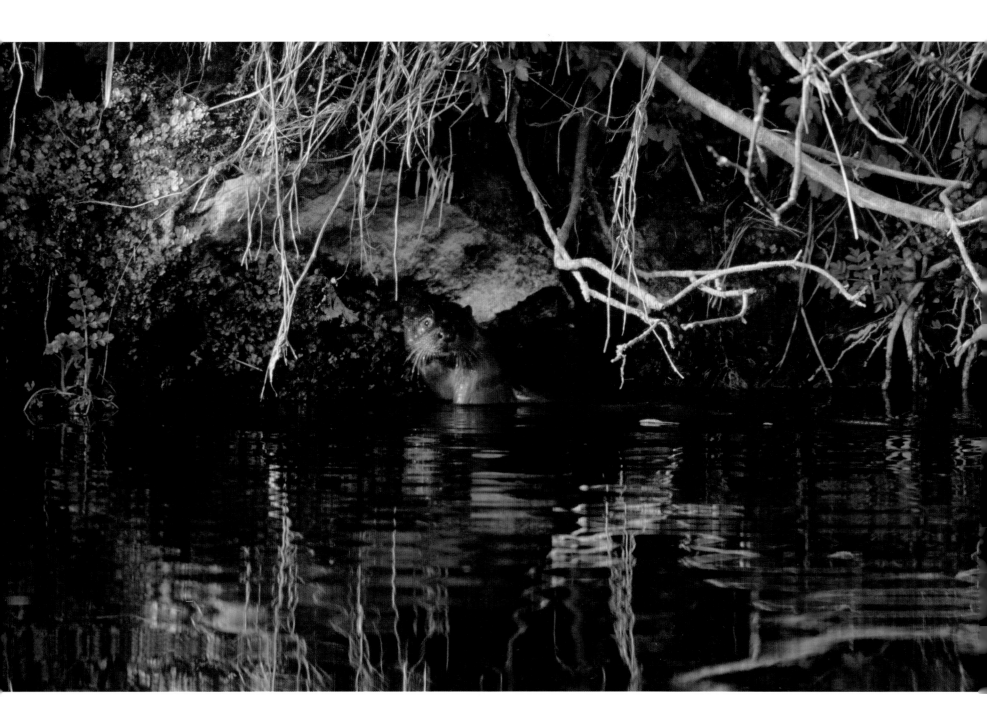

Chapter 6 Back on the Tweed

Late one May evening in 1993, Laurie was heading out with a friend to look for badgers in a wooded gully bordering the Tweed. It was a sett that Laurie had first discovered when he was a teenager and he'd watched many generations of badgers there. They were making their way along the dusky riverside path, still some distance from the wood, when they noticed a mallard suddenly fly up in alarm on the opposite bank. Laurie lifted his binoculars and slowly scanned the river's surface from bank to bank to see what had disturbed it. There in the distance, in the last of the light, he spotted something moving in the water, working its way alongside the bank, slipping in and out of the plants at the water's edge. There was just enough light to catch a glimpse of a small head and the arch of a sleek back before it disappeared from view.

It was enough to confirm what he had

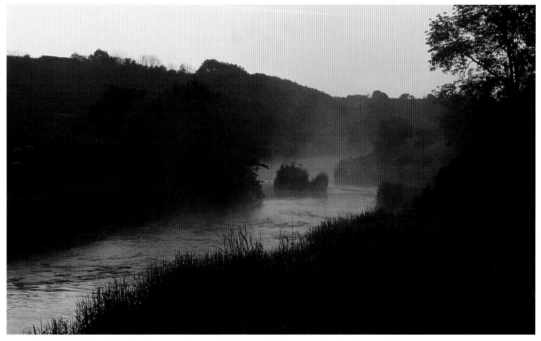

Opposite. An early benchmark photo – taken at 8.00 a.m., which was as late in the morning as I had ever seen an otter in the 1990s.

Above. Setting off at dawn – about 3.30 a.m. – in search of otters on the River Whiteadder.

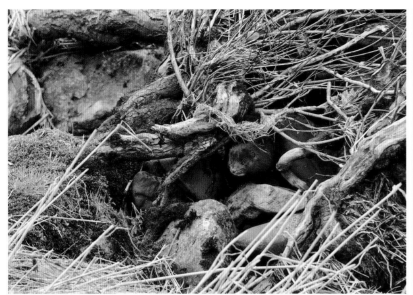

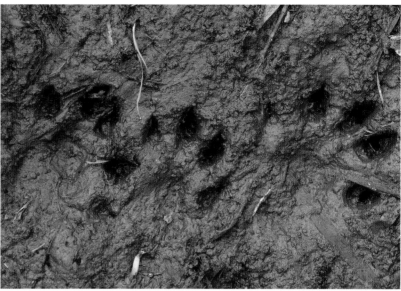

In the early days American mink were more widespread and many people would mistake them for otters.

The distinctive five-toed tracks of an otter – though often only four toes leave an impression.

barely dared to hope – otters had returned to the Tweed. The species that had enchanted him on so many visits to Scotland's west coast was now living right here on his own home river. There wasn't enough light to record that first encounter on camera, but it captured him and launched him on a new quest: to get acquainted with these river-dwelling otters and to create a photographic record of their lives.

Laurie wondered how long otters had been there before he first saw one, and whether he may have passed by their sleek forms in the dusky river, unknowingly. He had heard reports of otter sightings in the area but had taken them with a pinch of salt, presuming people had seen

feral American mink – which were more wide-spread at the time and were often misidentified. But now he remembered moments when he had heard something unseen on the riverbank – a sudden rustle in the rushes, a plop and a splash in the water, a sense of a large-ish, heavy animal moving away through the dense vegetation on the banks – had these been otters?

When another friend pointed out a small, dark mound of spraint on a rock in shallow water, Laurie realised why he may have missed the telltale signs of the otters' presence. After two decades of tracking otters in the West Highlands he was well acquainted with the field signs left by otters inhabiting the seashore. But

these river-dwelling otters seemed an altogether different beast. For a start, their diet wasn't the same, therefore neither was their spraint. He knew otter spraint from the shore – it looked kind of 'crunchy', full of little white bits that are the remains of crustaceans – and so had missed the spraint on the riverbank, which was smooth, black and tar-like. And while coastal otters are out and about in the daytime, their lives governed by the state of the tides, these river denizens slipped out at dawn and dusk, moving secretively in the half-light, easily melting into the dark river or disappearing into the river-bank.

'Getting your eye in' is a favourite expression

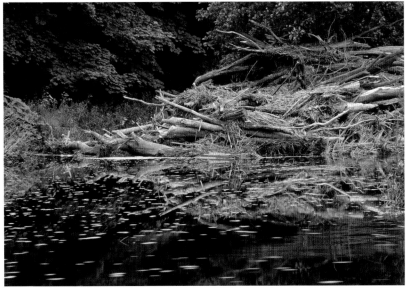

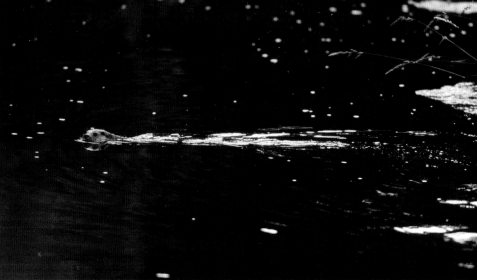

A log pile created by winter spates forms an ideal otter holt.

Leaving this holt in the last of the light – about 9.30 on a cloudy June evening.

of Laurie's; to him, it is the key to the process of learning to spot wildlife in its context, of the watery world coming into focus as you get a sense of scale and begin to discern the difference, for example, in splashes and ripples and the way the water's surface responds after being disturbed by a fish or a duck or an otter. He was going to have to go through the process of 'getting your eye in' all over again.

Now that he knew, he started to see the subtle signs of their presence more regularly, such as tracks in the mud by the water's edge, that dark spraint and flattened areas of grass on secluded patches of riverbank where otters would emerge to roll around and dry them-

selves. By watching silently, keeping downwind at quiet moments of dawn and dusk, he began to see the otters themselves more often.

Over time his search widened along the Tweed and its tributaries. As well as his own field craft, Laurie discovered where otters were present by talking to anyone he met who also spent time at the river at odd hours – dog walkers, joggers, anglers, salmon poachers and water bailiffs alike. He found signs of otters along the whole length of the river, high in the hills and right down to the brackish waters of the estuary.

He was delighted to find otters on Whiteadder Water, one of the Tweed's many tributaries

that flows down from the Lammermuir Hills and curves around behind his home village before joining the larger river near the estuary. Meandering through the Berwickshire landscape, the Whiteadder has stretches of steep-sided bank-side cut over millennia by the river, where peregrine falcons nest on exposed cliffs and where small pockets of native woodland remain. Living between the two rivers, he chose to spend more time watching the Whiteadder because it has a more intimate feel than the nearby Tweed, which is broader and tidal in its lower reaches.

On the Whiteadder, Laurie found an ideal site for a concentrated otter-watch: a quiet, wild

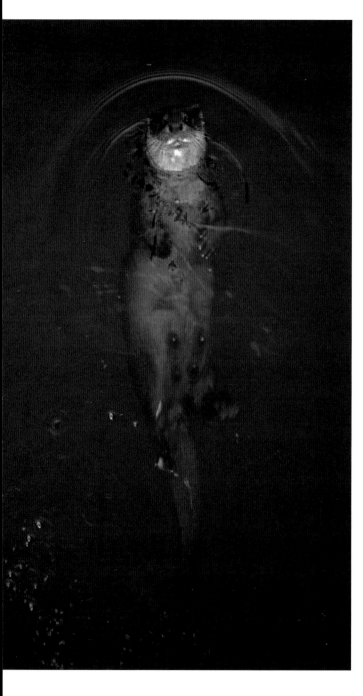

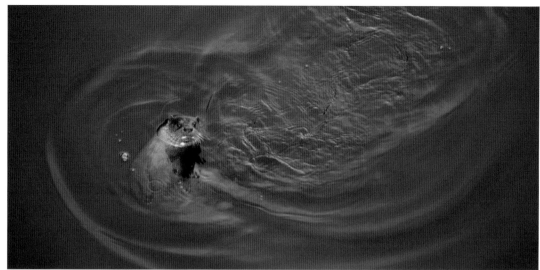

Looking down from a bridge I was well above the nose of this female otter, but still she stopped to check me out – giving me the unusual opportunity to photograph an otter upright in the water, and revealing her swollen nipples which showed she was suckling.

wooded place, where you would rarely see another person. It was the kind of secret, silent spot where roe deer like to lie up in the daytime. Within a few minutes walking distance from his home, Laurie watched this site religiously and began to see otters more regularly. As these first sightings were mostly at night and occasionally in the half-light of dusk and dawn, photography was almost impossible. But still he watched, learning to get the scale of an otter's head in the new context of this landscape and to discern the sleek form of a rolling brown otter against the rolling brown river.

Gradually, Laurie began to recognise individual otters through their distinctive markings and scars, including a female with a pale patch

of fur on her chin. He watched her raise her cubs two years in succession from a holt that he discovered hidden in a pile of woody debris that had washed down the river and lodged in the remains of a weir.

This was a long-term project, stretching over years, steadily accumulating observations, testing techniques by trial and error and building a body of knowledge about the otters' lives and how to photograph them. Laurie had to work around the demands of other projects, sometimes frustrated to be interrupted by the call of a trip to the north when he was engrossed by the rivers at home. When he had the opportunity to watch certain areas intensively, he came to recognise other individual animals, to

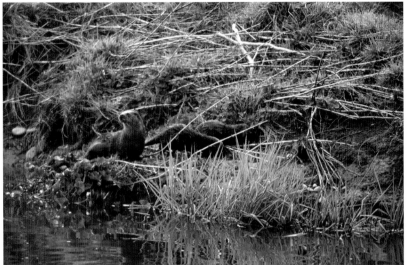
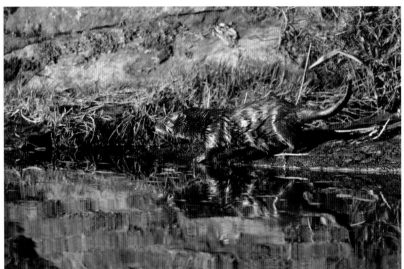

I recognised this same female otter by the white patch on her throat, she lived with her two cubs in the log-pile holt (p. 99).

One of 'white throat's' cubs takes to the river in the early morning sunlight.

know the patterns of their days and the boundaries of their territories. One spring he watched two females with young cubs that lived less than a mile apart and he noticed how they set off in opposite directions each evening so as not to cross into each other's territory. He got to know favoured feeding spots, homing in on rocky areas where the otters would root around, nudging the rocks to disturb small fish beneath.

The more he learnt about the otters' lives and habitat, the more opportunities for photography arose. In summer he would often be out on the riverbank before five in the morning. The otters might still have been out and about and feeding in the first light, but they would then be heading back to their holts by seven or eight o'clock, when the rest of the human world was waking up. Some nights he slept out on the riverbank, stirring in the first light to see an otter gliding past beside him, or hearing the peeping call in the darkness that confirmed the presence of cubs.

Laurie developed a range of strategies to get himself into the right position for the photographs. Sometimes he would settle into a recess in the riverbank, wearing camouflage clothing, including dark gloves and face netting. Other times he would hang over a bridge, ready and waiting for otters passing underneath. He would note exactly when the shadow of the bridge left the pool of deep water below, so as to maximise the chances of being in the right place at the right time to catch his subject swimming below in the clear morning light.

He became aware of the different modes of swimming that otters would adopt: purposefully travelling when returning to their holts after a prolonged hunting and feeding session; loitering and investigating when feeding; and the arching, looping, splashing of play and courtship. Otters are powerful swimmers and can cover quite a distance when they're on the move. It can be a challenge to keep up with them on a riverbank, especially when laden with photographic equipment. The trick, then, is to get ahead of the animal and to lie in wait. Sometimes Laurie would don chest waders and wait in the middle of the river. The otters seemed less

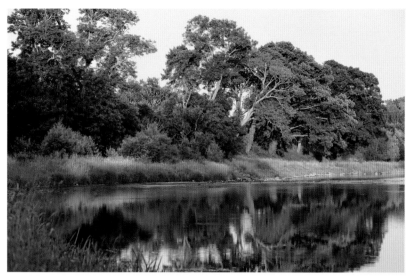

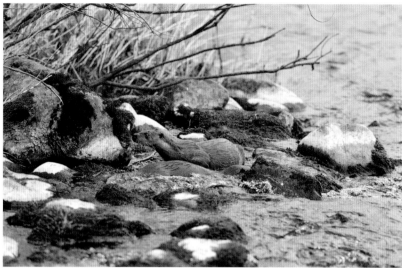

A still, summer's evening on the River Teviot as I set out otter watching. So much has changed since the early days of the project.

The otters are less wary and more often seen in the daytime, and I had learnt to see an otter (or two) at a glance along the rocky riverbank.

concerned by a low form in the water than a tall shape on the bank.

Many 'otter tracking' skills were transferable from coast to river. An awareness of the animal's keen senses was paramount. This meant keeping a low profile below the skyline, using a backdrop of trees or rock or riverbank to disguise the shape of a human silhouette from the otter's eye view. He also paid close attention to the wind direction and would not approach an otter when the wind was behind him, in case it betrayed his unfamiliar scent to the otter's acute sense of smell.

There was a certain etiquette, Laurie discovered, to riverside otter watching. With appropriate behaviour and keeping at a certain distance, the otters might know he was there but would be comfortable with his presence. He often felt as if he were being monitored in some way. An otter would regularly glance in his direction and then, when satisfied he wasn't doing anything too strange or threatening, it would simply carry on with whatever it was doing.

As the years went by, Laurie noticed a steady increase in otter numbers throughout the Tweed River System, and a gradual change in behaviour. There was no doubt the otters were getting bolder, becoming more active in daylight and more tolerant of limited disturbance. In the early days of the project, they were utterly elusive and virtually nocturnal, melting back into the river and disappearing completely at the slightest disturbance by a strange sight, sound or scent. More than two decades later it's not unusual to see otters out fishing in the daytime, aware of but unperturbed by people passing by. Fishermen building a landing stage were regularly 'visited' by a curious otter as they worked, and in one Borders town, which the Tweed loops around like a bypass, CCTV cameras have revealed otters taking a short cut right through the town centre at night. On busy stretches of river, where the road passes close by or the riverside paths are well used by walkers and fishermen, the regular comings and goings of people had become part of the otter's familiar landscape. Successive generations of

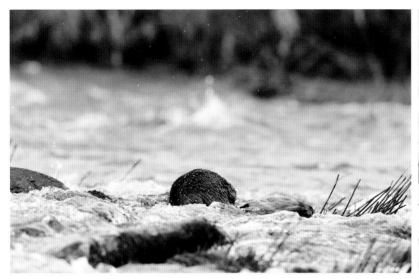

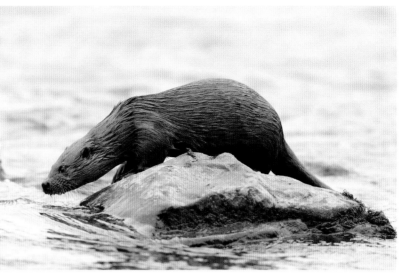

And to spot the difference between the sleek, rounded hump of an otter's back and the rocks around it.

This work had begun with distant glimpses in the dusk, and now I could photograph a whole otter out of the water in the daylight.

otters were growing up in these sites accustomed to human presence, realising nothing bad was happening and so becoming less wary than their predecessors.

These changes in otter behaviour increased and enhanced the opportunities for photography. By a happy coincidence, photography itself was rapidly developing through this time. The advent of digital photography created cameras that could record images in marginal lighting conditions, opening up a whole new range of possibilities for working further into either end of the day – just when the otters were active.

This serendipitous combination of changes in both subject and medium has assisted Laurie with his quest. And now, twenty years since he first glimpsed an otter on the Tweed, he has amassed thousands of hours of otter watches and taken as many photographs. It's time for the pictures to tell their story – of these lithe, fierce, graceful carnivores claiming the river once more, of their mornings out fishing, their calls to their cubs and their tracks in the snow, of the plants and birdlife and other animals that are an inextricable part of their habitat and of the morning mist and evening light that envelopes their world.

Yet this work is not finished, and never will be. Laurie will always want one more season, one more year, to capture another aspect of behaviour or to re-shoot a scene in a new light. He's got many more pictures in his mind's eye, some are scenes that he has witnessed but not yet managed to photograph, others are of things he hasn't yet seen but knows they occur: an otter sliding in the snow; rolling itself dry inside a hollow log; or, that holy grail of wild otter photography – a *dry* otter!

The need to realise the pictures in his mind, to make them tangible, is what drives Laurie to get out of bed before four in the morning, or to stay up all night on the riverbank, or to hold out for one more hour on a bitterly cold winter's day. These images will continue to inspire and frustrate him, to distract him from whatever else he is working on and compel him time and time again to return to the river.

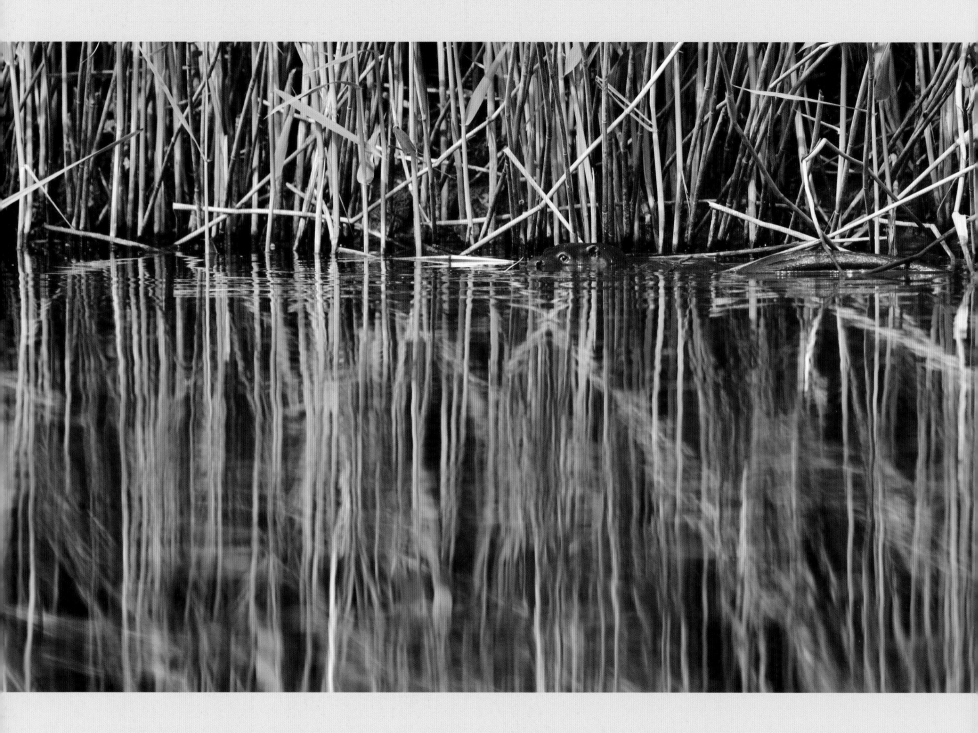

Reeds

It's 6 a.m. and bright already. I'd expected a softer tint of morning light, but the colours of the river and trees below me are all precise in the clear daylight. I'm waiting for Laurie on the bridge and scanning the river with my binoculars, looking for otter clues. He appears behind me, tripod over his shoulder, beanbag around his waist. He's spent the night on the riverbank, falling asleep to the sound of the river rushing by, and waking at 4 a.m. to see an otter swimming past – a sleek head on the water, dark against the morning light on the surface. But the otter was heading downstream, travelling purposefully back to its holt. It could have done its fishing already and be heading home to sleep through the day. Laurie's looking worried, are we too late already?

We scan the river from both sides of the bridge, then set off to try our luck further along the riverside path, where sunlight is streaming through the trees. The vegetation is lush and thick along the banks, so dense you can't see through to the river, though you can hear its constant babble. But there are gaps, like windows framed with green, and we stop and scan the river at each one.

I'd imagined that accompanying Laurie would involve long hours of sitting still in silence, but mostly I'm trying to keep up; he covers a lot of ground with a long stride. For a guy who can spend more than 35 hours cramped in a tiny eagle hide on a cliff side, he seems barely able to sit still. He just pauses, crouches down sometimes, listens, scans, and then strides on. When you've 'got your eye in' to that extent, a glance is all it takes to detect an otter's head low on the water, or a trail of bubbles, or a sudden splash, to make the decision whether to wait and watch or to move on.

We move on, striding through the green corridor, spotlights of sunshine sneaking through the canopy and leaving quivering circles of light on the path as we walk. I'm resisting the urge to jump between them.

'See that otter?' Laurie has reached the next window. Then I see it, too. A tail, then a hump, then a raised lump of body, in and out of the rocks. A sleek, dark, fluid shape as if a bit of the river itself is moving along the bank. Then it loops and rolls and the long tail waves as it pushes into the water. Then it vanishes. A mallard family come pootling along, six young ducklings following each other, seeming unconcerned and with no sign of alarm or indication that there's a fierce predator close by. We wait and watch and Laurie scans his expert scan, but it's gone. Utterly gone, leaving no trace. As if the otter were just a river spirit, taking form momentarily and then dissolving back into the water and becoming river again. Laurie points to a sparrow-hawk overhead; it glints in the sunlight.

We move on upstream, hoping for a longer encounter and the opportunity to photograph it. We're changed by the glimpse of otter, uplifted now and walking alert and full of hope as we peer round each twist and turn in the river. The enchanted corridor opens out as we follow the river's gentle curves. Here willows are stretching over the water and the air is full of birdsong and river chatter. I start at sudden splashes midstream, but it's only fish jumping. You'd think otters would plop and splash, and fish would be silent and mysterious, and it makes me smile that it's the other way round.

Some miles upstream we reach a small weir. The river's very low here, dancing and bubbling around moss-covered rocks. Laurie says this is where he'd settle if he had the chance to spend twenty-four hours in one spot by the riverside. He'd had a successful encounter here the year before – had taken some of the best images – and the scene of such a meeting seems to hold its enchantment, the landscape imprinted with blessed memories. But it's past nine o'clock now, and the sun is bright and hot. We'll just linger for a moment, then call it a day, head back to the motorhome for breakfast and cups of tea and . . .

'There's an otter.' As if on cue. As Laurie says the

words, he's already down on the ground, adjusting lenses, keeping low. I follow his gaze to the opposite bank, where the reeds are moving and twitching. Then I see it, almost flat in the river, just where the streaks of yellow and green reeds meet their reflections in the water. I can make out a head, a low length of body and a long, flat tail floating like a twig on the surface.

There's a small path leading down from our main path through the long grass to the river, and we follow it down and settle amongst the plants by the water's edge. While Laurie swiftly organises tripod, cameras and lenses, I watch through my binoculars. The otter rolls itself into the water, then comes bursting up; it has caught something and is chomping down on it, throwing its head back and opening its mouth wide and biting down. Then it rolls and loops again.

Laurie's got a fancy gadget, an eye-piece that attaches to the camera lens, effectively turning it into a powerful telescope. I take a look through it and gasp. The otter is astoundingly close. I can see its long whiskers . . . and its white dagger teeth as it bites . . . the spikes of fur on its head and the almost pinkish underside of its cream throat . . .

It rolls underwater, then the head erupts surprisingly far out of the water, then the body loops where the head was, then there's just a tail, which flicks and curves and waves, a lithe, eel-like creature with a life of its own. A head bursts up again, where the tail was. I wonder for a moment if there's more than one animal there.

It's rummaging – rummaging at the base of the reeds, sometimes flicking stones up or dislodging bits of wood that float around on the surface. Then it surfaces with the fur on its face all muddy spikes. Then dives and pounces again. We're trying to figure what it's feeding on, something small, but it's difficult to see what. And we're trying to think of the word for when pigs do that kind of rummaging. Then we chuckle when we find it – truffling – such an undignified, un-ottery word for such a graceful creature, but still, our otter is truffling in the reed bed.

The reeds are a gift, holding our otter in the frame and keeping it diving on the same spot. I alternate between my binoculars and naked eye, watching the brown shape bobbing and looping, the streaky, straw-like vertical layers of colour in the reeds, the yellow of the fields behind and the blue sky beyond that. When I lose sight of the otter for a moment, the reeds twitch obligingly to reveal where it is feeding.

A jogger in a cerise top comes pounding and panting along the path opposite us, oblivious to the wild animal hidden on the other side of the reed bed. The otter glances up but continues its chomping and looping and truffling, unconcerned by the thudding footsteps.

On and on and on it feeds and rummages, loops and swirls, turns and dives, bursts out of the water and twists back in again, working its way slowly along the reed bed. An hour passes by. It seems to know we're there, shoots the occasional glance in our direction, but is not troubled by our presence. We move downstream a bit to get ahead of it and into a good position to take photographs should it reach the end of the reed bed and decide to leave the water and come up onto the grassy bank – Laurie is still after photographs of a whole otter, as most of the time in the water you see just the top of the head and back and tail.

Then there's a human shout and a collie comes bounding down the path, barking. It hasn't seen the otter, just two strange human forms crouching low in the long grass by the water's edge. It woofs at us, then gallops into the water, then doubles back to investigate us, all wet fur and wagging tail and hot breath.

An apologetic owner retrieves the dog and hauls it back. We look to the other bank, but our otter has vanished. We wait and watch for a while, but she's gone. We scan the river. The only movement is the water leaping and dancing over the weir and the sunlight playing on the water.

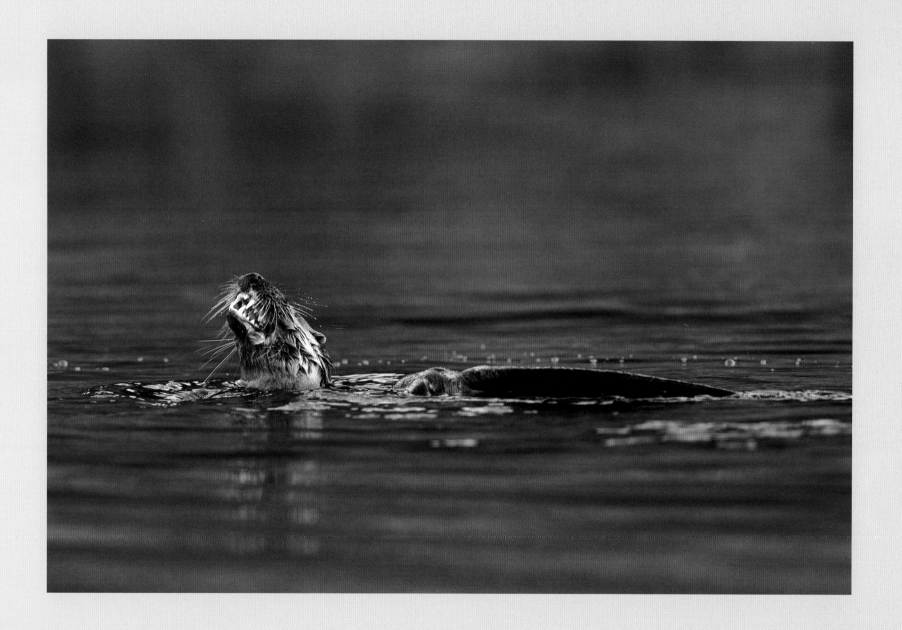

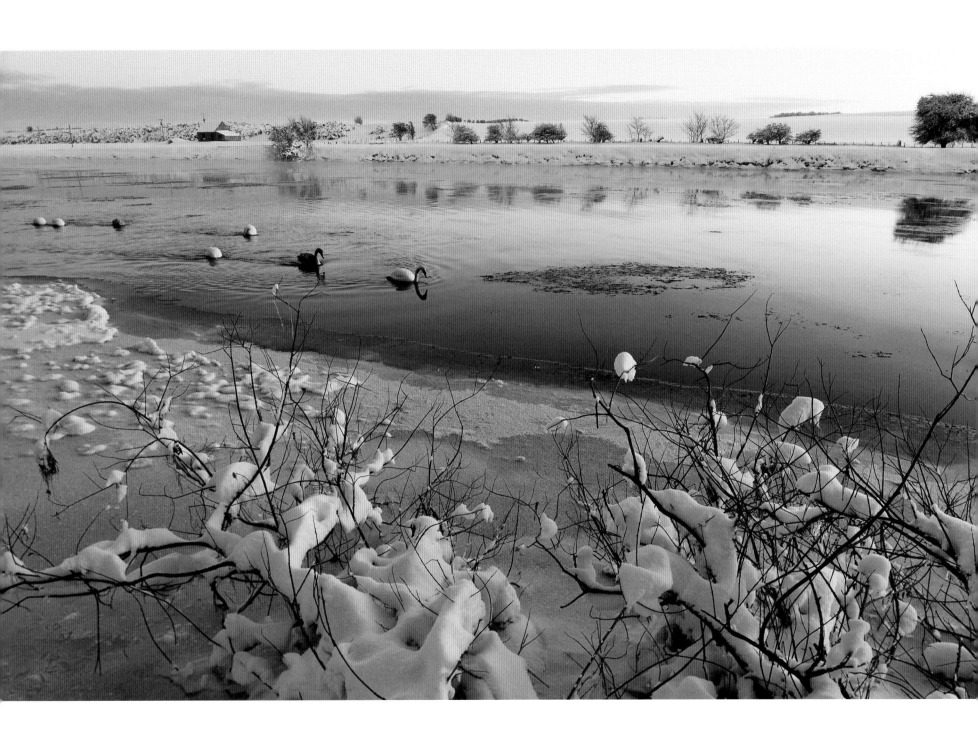

Chapter 7 Winter

Winter brings a whole new world of opportunity for wildlife watching and photography. Just as the skeleton trees reveal the birdlife in their branches, so the lack of vegetation on the riverbank makes it easier to spot a sleek creature slipping in or out of the water. While winter weather has its challenges, even the worst conditions can be put to good use for photography, and the advantages of working in the cold are well worth any discomfort. Heavy falls of snow can create magical lighting conditions, acting as a giant wrap-around reflector, enveloping everything in soft, uncomplicated lighting. Clear skies at night cause temperatures to plummet, resulting in mist rising from the surface of rivers at sunrise and early morning frosts that turn simple leaves and grasses into exquisite opportunities for close-up photography.

On the banks of the Whiteadder it's quiet before the human fishing season begins on the first of February, but the otters are already feeding well on early runs of salmon and sea trout. By February and March, there's a sense of anticipation, waiting for the young otter cubs to emerge from their holts, and for the otters' story to begin again.

This scene may be at least five miles from the sea, but it is tidal at this point and this brackish water can still freeze. I was walking along the riverside, following this family party of mute swans as they headed upstream to roost, feeding along the way. This image looks so still and quiet with the magenta and blue glow of the light on the snow, but when I look at it I can hear the sounds of that winter day. The frozen river grinds and cracks as the tide turns. And the sounds of the swans – the feint squeaks of their calls and the gentle tapping of their bills dabbling in the water.

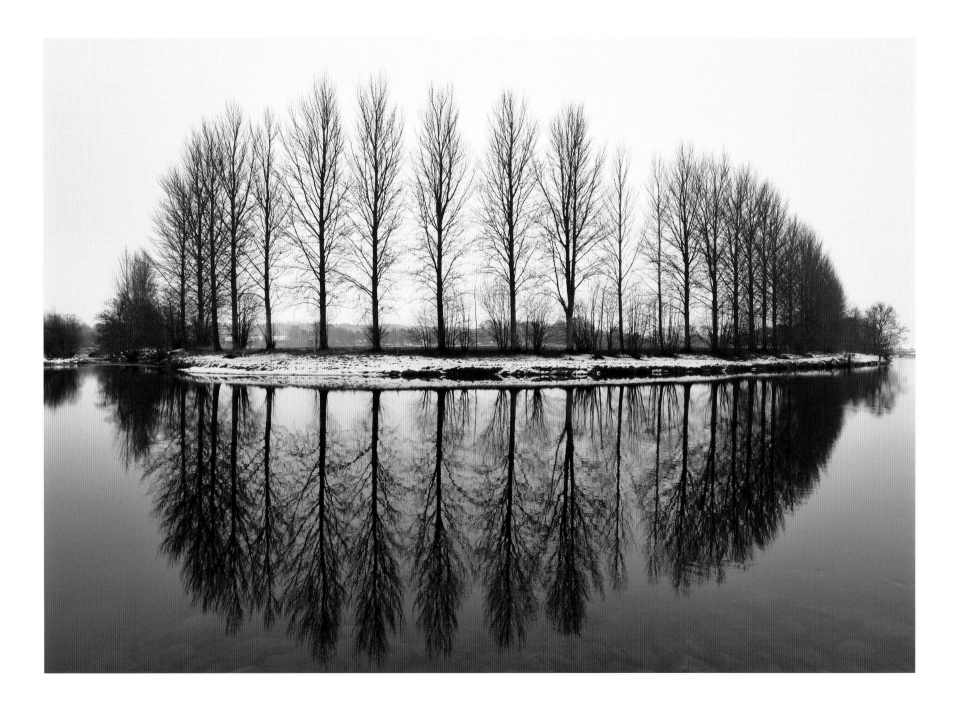

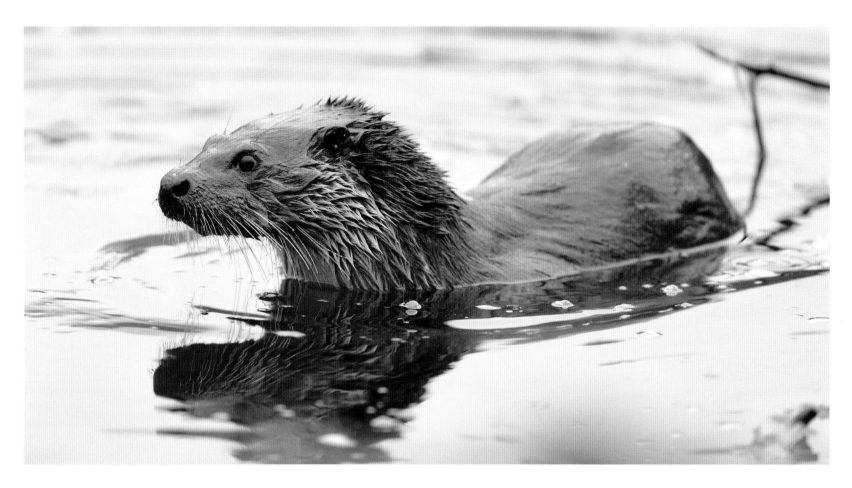

It was flat calm on the Teviot this February day; not a ripple on the water. There was a tangible stillness, as if the river was holding its breath. The conditions that allowed me to capture the perfect symmetry of this arc of winter trees are also ideal for otter spotting. It's much easier to notice any disturbance on the surface on an overcast day when the water is a uniform grey than on a bright sunny day, with its sharp contrasts and shadows. Sound carries very well over still water, too. Not that otters make a lot of noise – they're remarkably silent and stream-lined – but on a day like this you could hear the occasional soft splash, or later in the spring the high-pitched peeping of contact calls between cubs and their mother. After winter spates, the river has churned up all sorts of mud and debris, and the water is rarely clear. I've watched otters fishing in water the consistency of drinking chocolate and can't imagine they can see much in there, so they must be using their sensitive whiskers, as well as scent, to detect their prey. The muddy water enhanced this otter's 'wet gel' look, sticking its sleek fur into punky spikes.

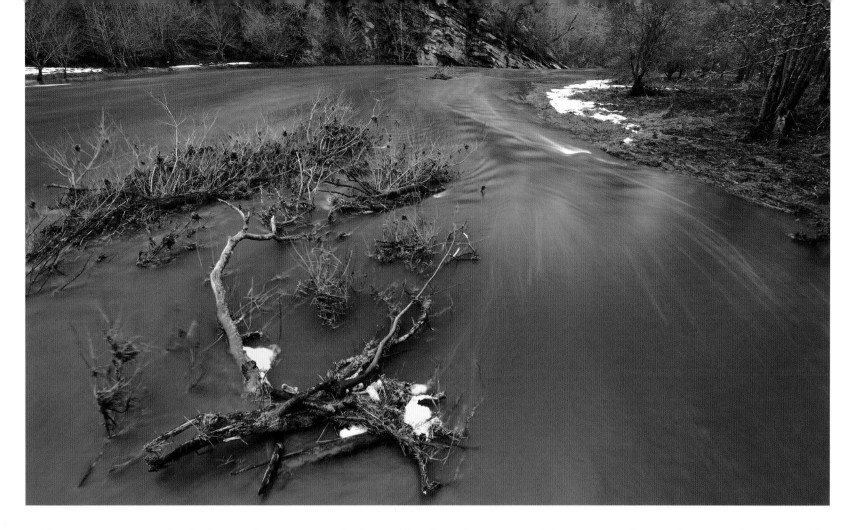

Mild, wet winters bring floods that send the river levels soaring, bursting their banks. The Whiteadder was enormous this morning, swollen and surging, sweeping up whole branches and carrying them downstream. Woody debris like this accumulates where the river levels are high; it all gets carried along and eventually gets caught up and deposited somewhere along the riverbank. Some river authorities remove this to clean up the river, but I think we need to be careful and wonder if this should be a licensed activity, as I've often found evidence of otter holts where this debris collects and forms shelter on the riverbank. Besides, there are the obvious benefits to the life in the river itself, with the input of this organic material. When the river is hurtling along like this, I wonder about the mortality of young cubs, especially with bank-side holts – can the mothers cope? And where do they go? On the coast, mothers and cubs can be separated by rough seas; this must be the river's equivalent to a rough sea in terms of the sheer force of the water.

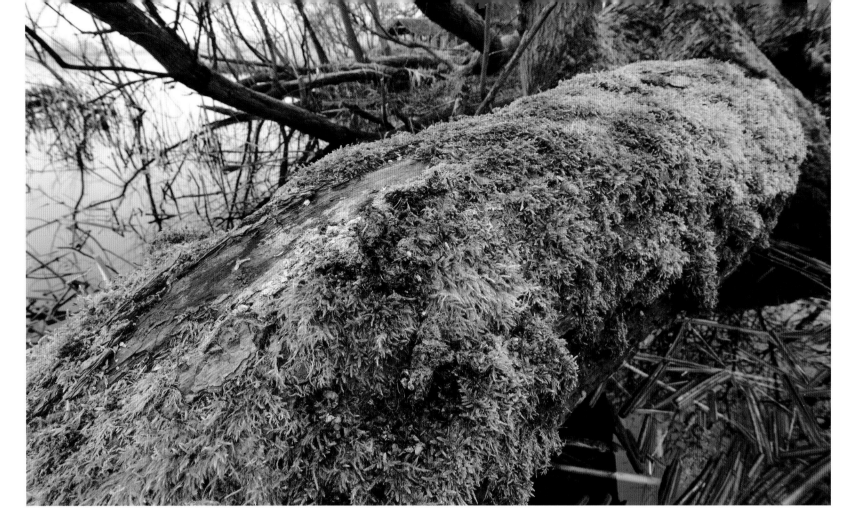

Sometimes I get an idea in my mind's eye and go to great lengths to realise it with a photograph. After investing a lot of time and effort preparing and waiting for a particular shot, I get to the stage that I feel if I pack it in it's all been for nothing. But then, of course, there's tremendous satisfaction when you do get that picture. Many of these ideas are still very much 'work in progress'. For example, I created a high seat up on the leaning bough of a mature willow where I've spent many, many hours looking down on this sculptural tangle of branches and trees on the shore of a loch below. Simply seeing fresh spraint there regularly makes my spirits soar! It's almost as good as seeing an otter – it means they're here, and I'm alert with expectation. Otters are clearly using this willow regularly as a territorial scent marker – you can see the mounds of fresh spraint and the brown patches where the accumulation of urine has burnt the moss. I've seen otters passing by on the water, but I'm still watching, and waiting, to see them climbing around here on their way to the 'toilet' –I haven't caught them yet.

Another photograph on my wish list is to catch an otter drying itself inside the pipes formed by fallen, decaying hollow trees. Inside, you can see where they have been smoothed by otters rolling around, using the dry, fibrous material like a wrap-around bath towel.

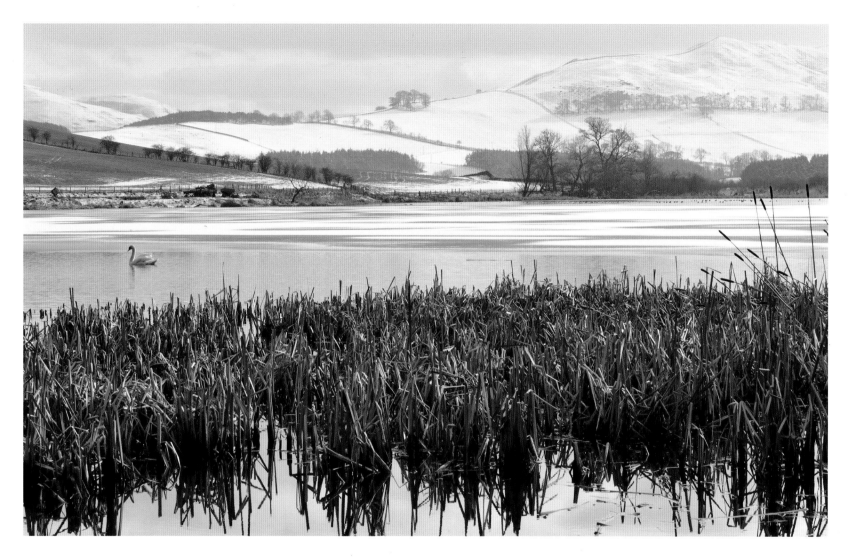

Watching bodies of still water in winter is a good bet for an otter sighting – the distances can be greater than the breadth of the river, but my dream image here at Yetholm Loch is of an otter running over the surface of the frozen water. I haven't got it yet, but I've photographed many other subjects while waiting for it.

When the loch isn't frozen, the otters tend to work around the water's edge, and they can be difficult to spot as they rummage around the reeds and marshy areas. I can't follow the otters as I do on the river; it's more about just being content to settle down at a spot that offers a commanding view. The hide overlooking the water is a perfect place to do just that. I've spent many a comfortable winter's day there, cosseted in my down-filled sleeping bag, with a flask of peppermint tea, just watching and waiting.

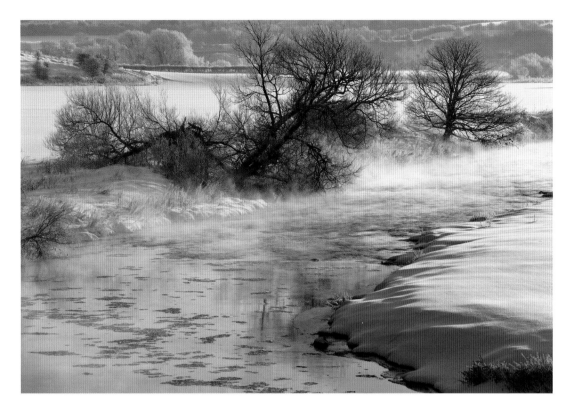

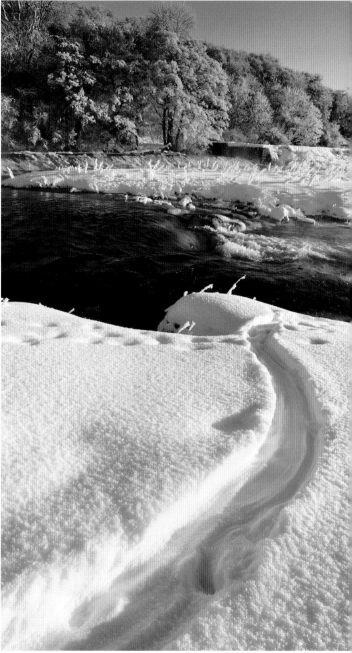

Deep snow is a rare event in our maritime climate in south-east Scotland. So when it happens – as it did over two exceptionally cold recent winters – it's extra special and can lead to many new discoveries for me. Heavy snowfall is a gift for tracking otters – aspects of their lives that had escaped my notice were revealed by the snow. I found otter tracks many miles from the water, showing the distance that otters will travel across country to take a short cut from one river to another. I had assumed otters would stick to a watery route: following one river until they reached the confluence and then going up the other river. I also came across this slide made by the otters. However, an image of an otter sliding down it is still on my wish list! The temperature this day was down below -10°C and for four consecutive days I sat by the riverside from eight in the morning until six in the evening hoping for that moment. At least these days I have specialised equipment, so that I can be comfy in these conditions. Top of my list are my neoprene-lined 'winter wellies' and a down jacket. I always believe that the more comfortable you are, the longer you'll be inclined to wait – and the longer you wait, the more you'll see.

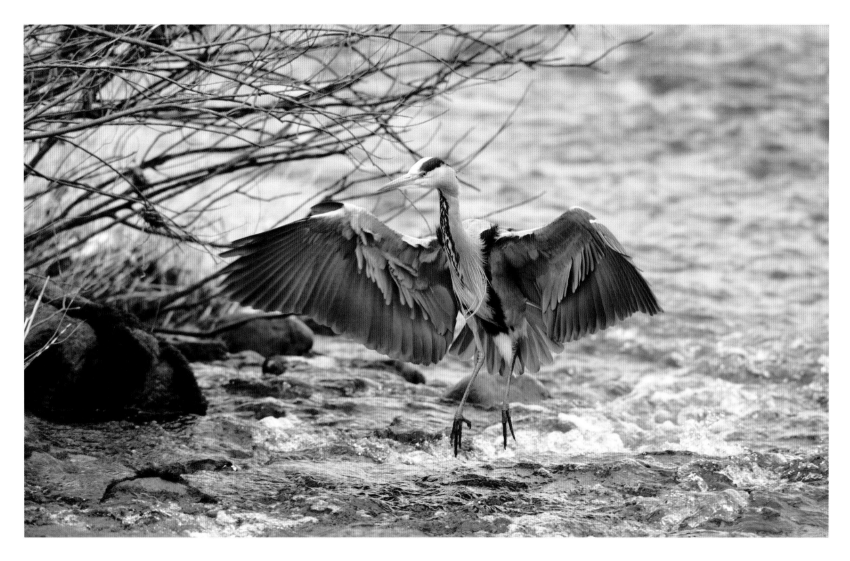

I'm often asked if I have a favourite subject to photograph. I don't really, but if pressed I would be tempted to say the grey heron. These herons have been a constant on the river all my life and their stately presence, like sculptures on the riverbank, somehow changes the atmosphere and adds a richer dimension to the scene. In my early days of photography, herons were my focus – they're strikingly attractive and photogenic. They're also very inspiring. Watching them feeding, I realise it's all about patience – they're not like waders, darting or rummaging around; they just wait. They are territorial and I hear their croaking, guttural calls as they squabble over favoured hunting grounds. That's their strategy: find a location that they know works, and watch and wait for as long as it takes – a bit like nature photography, really.

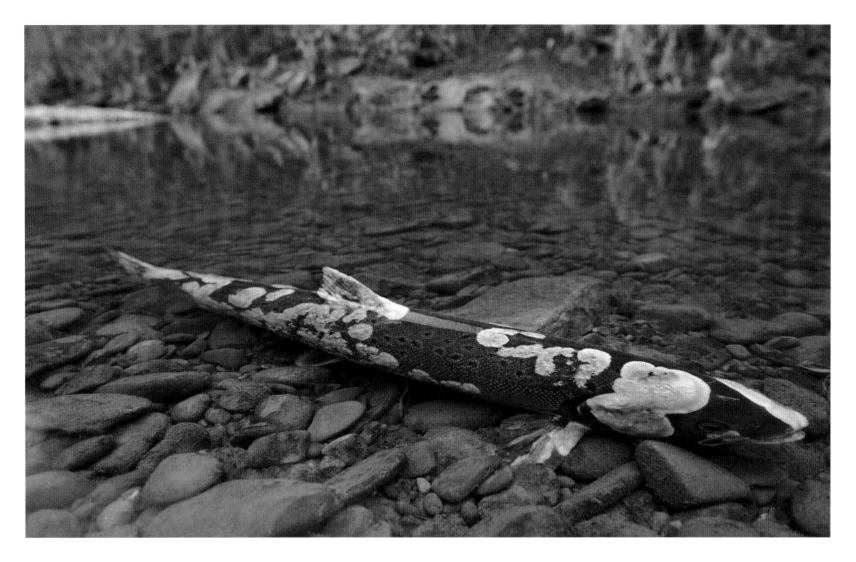

'Spent' salmon, known as kelts, are to me symbolic of this time of year. They have spawned in late autumn, laying their eggs in the gravel riverbeds (or 'redds') upstream and now they've come back down the river, exhausted and vulnerable. In this weakened state, they're susceptible to disease – the white patches on this fish are from the fungal disease ulcerative dermal necrosis (UDN). It dulls their senses, making them easy prey for a surprising range of other wildlife. I've even seen signs of badgers having waded into shallow woodland streams after them, and crows having a go, too. They're easy pickings for an otter.

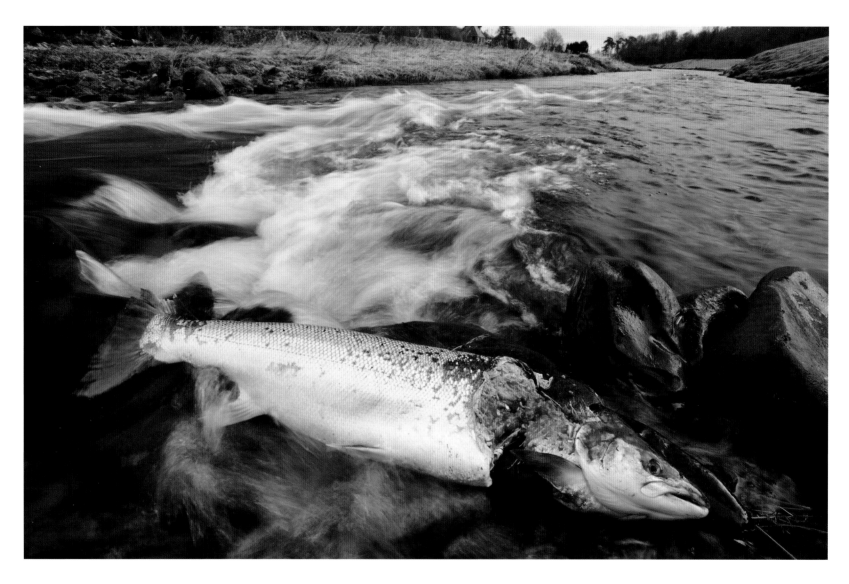

Sometimes the otters will eat their fill, starting from around the gill area and leaving the rest of the fish. Crows will have a go at any remains while it is daylight, and then the nightshift comes: foxes and badgers scavenge what is left.

On this occasion I couldn't resist scavenging the otter's leftovers myself. By the time I'd cleaned it up, I had nine pounds of salmon – more than enough to feed the family of four for two nights.

On one occasion I found such a partly eaten fish halfway across a field – with a trail of scales and blood leading from the river. There must have been quite a battle!

Once I watched an otter struggling with a huge fish. I thought it was close to landing it, so

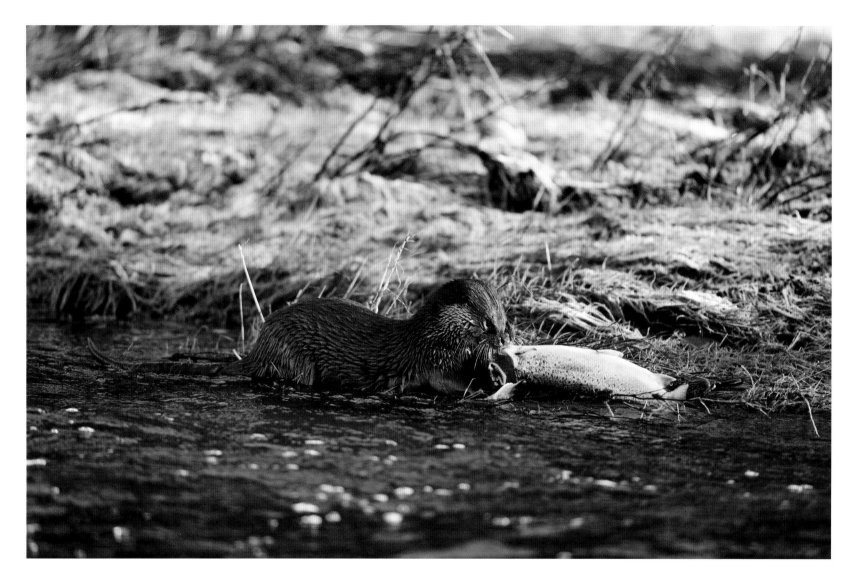

I decided to hide and wait until it had brought the fish to the bank, and then creep up and photograph it. But that never happened: the fish must have been a good twenty-pounder and it was writhing away; the otter lost its footing and the two of them then hurtled down the channel right beneath me, rolling over and over in the current. It would have made an incredible shot, but the long lens I had fitted to my camera at the time only had a minimum focusing distance of five metres and they were still too close to me. Eventually, the otter lost its hold and the fish got away.

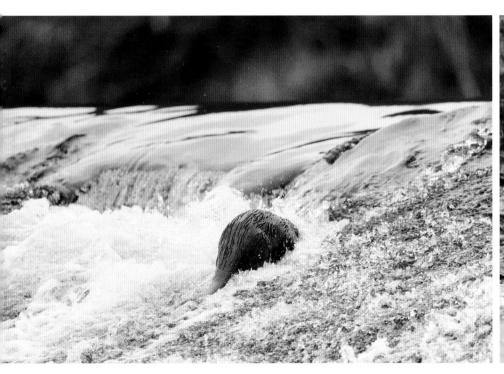 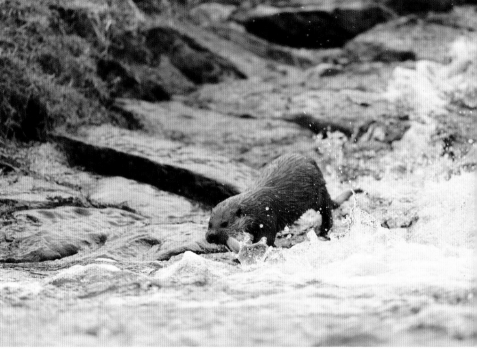

Once they'd discovered it, the otters frequently targeted this pool beneath the weir to feed on the salmon and trout. It was an ideal location for them, and for me – this small recess in the riverbank gave me a place to hide below the skyline. With a tree trunk dragged into position to form a barrier between myself and my subjects, I completed my camouflage with a head net and gloves to cover my pale skin, so I could settle there undetected. This otter was behaving oddly, rummaging in amongst the stonework of the weir, where it seemed there was a small step or ledge. I realised the fish were stalled there, struggling to get up the weir because the water levels were low from a lack of

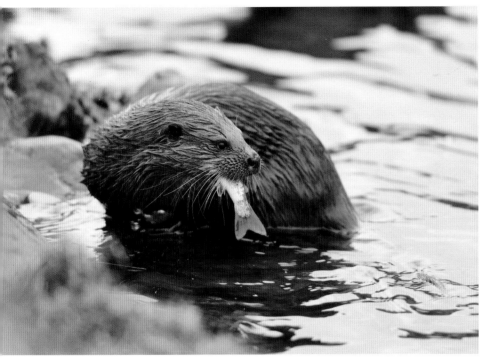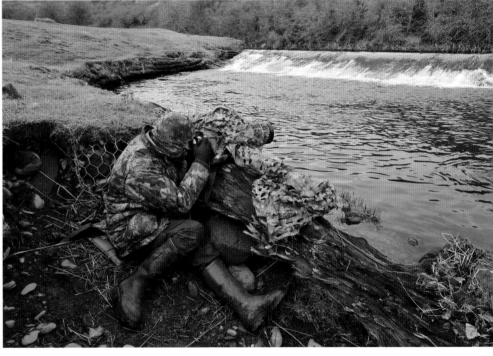

rain. Settled in my hiding place, I watched as it grabbed a brown trout before disappearing into the pool at the bottom of the weir, only to pop up moments later, where it landed its catch, just seven feet from me. It was much too close for my big lens, but I had a second camera fitted with a shorter lens for back-up and was able to lean over and photograph it before it finished its meal.

Another advantage of this location is that the noise of the rushing water on the weir masks the sound of the camera.

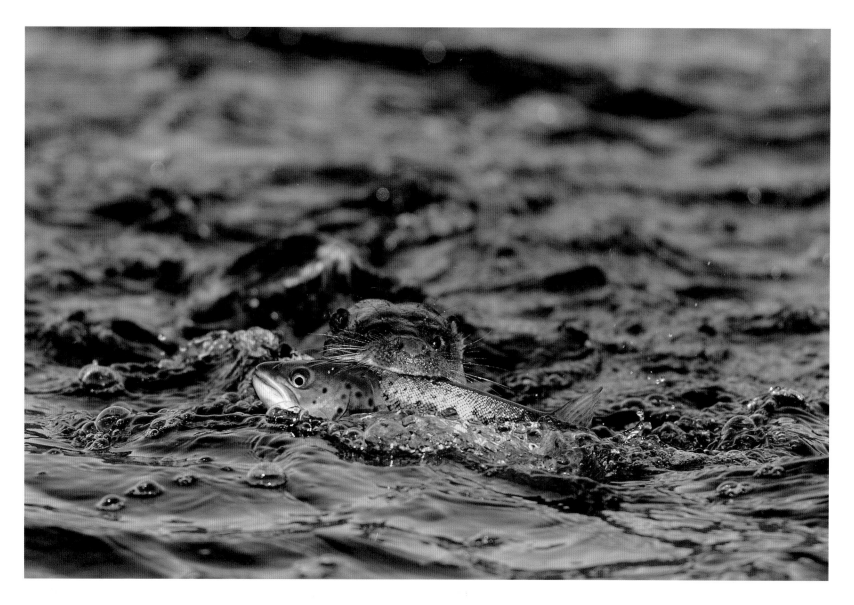

For some weeks in January, I watched from a distance as the otters landed fish of this impressive size. They'll eat small catches in the water but have to land anything big before they can feed. Suddenly this otter surfaced and swam straight towards me with a sea trout in its jaws. It was in view for less than five seconds before it saw me, then dived and took off to an island in the river to eat its catch. My camera may fire at nine frames a second, but I just had time to focus and capture three images.

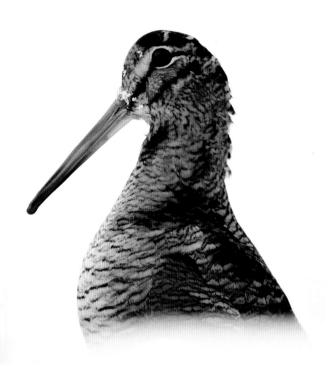

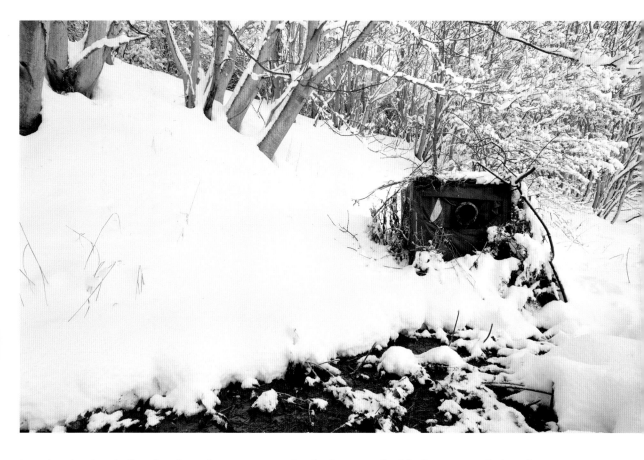

During the very cold winter of 2010, I erected a hide in some sheltered woodland behind our village. The area has a little microclimate and a spring that erupts in the wood creating a marshy area, which never really freezes, even when the surface of the Tweed is solid. I knew the cold conditions would attract the shy, secretive woodcock that needs soft ground in which to probe for invertebrate prey. My hide was pitched in the middle of the marsh and I spent three days sitting out the hours of light in a sleeping bag in four-by-three-foot area with all my kit. I saw nothing. Once the weather became even colder, I moved it to a drier place with a better view and tried again, settling into the hide by 3 a.m. The snow was so deep I couldn't drive to the location so I waded through the snow to enter then hide in darkness, these birds are so observant that I knew I mustn't 'taint' the hide with my presence if I wanted to use it again. So I'd have to see the whole stretch of daylight through from beginning to end – it's the same technique I use with eagles to ensure I'm not seen on the hill. In the end it all came down to one blessed day – I watched the dawn break and the woodcock slowly emerged just where I needed them to be, at one point I had six birds in view together. I got a landmark set of pictures that day – a 'red letter' day for me, and I felt I'd earned it.

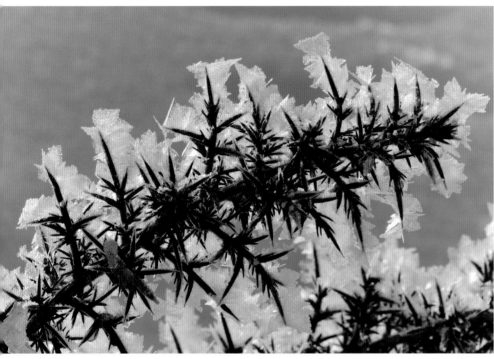

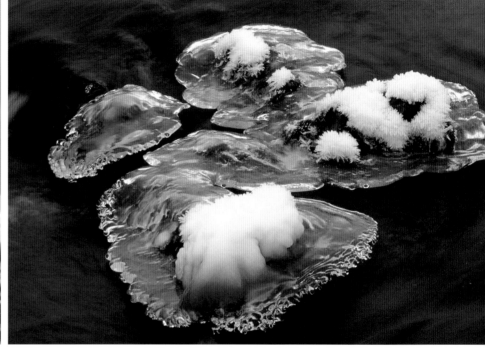

I spend a lot of time waiting beside water, and don't always see otters, but even when I do, I rarely manage to photograph everything I see – as happens with any form of photography. To pass the time while I'm waiting, I'm always looking out for other things to photograph in nature and these are usually the smallest details, like this hoar frost frozen onto gorse,

or the way the stones in the burn became encased in ice one bitterly cold night. There's always a therapeutic value in coming back with pictures of something, even if it isn't the subject you intended.

Simply watching otters capture prey while I follow them is fine, but I rarely know when this might happen – and then there is the problem

of getting close before they quickly devour the prey. Far better to lie in wait at a likely fishing spot. Keeping an eye on the bigger picture so often leads you to the target species. It was goosanders – these handsome diving ducks – which gave me a real breakthrough with my otter work. I'd long known, for example, that over the winter months goosanders frequented

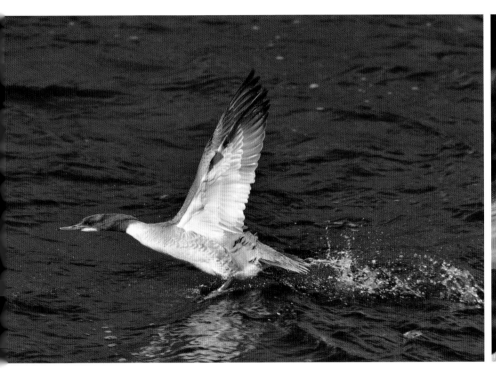
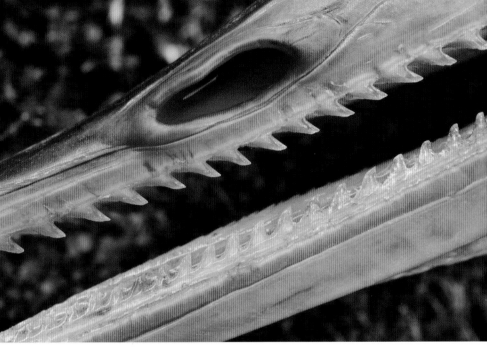

pools beneath weirs that once powered one of the many oat mills on the River Whiteadder. I realised the link between their presence and the early runs of salmon and sea trout, which were stacking up there, waiting to negotiate the falls, so they could move upstream to spawn. And, being so full of fish, this pool was likely to be popular with otters, too.

I see dead goosanders now and then, and I'm pretty sure they've been shot. They are seen as competition by some fishermen and, although quotas and culling licenses are issued each year, I have a sneaking suspicion that limits are exceeded and nobody is counting just how many are really killed.

Goosanders are members of the 'sawbill'

family, which also includes mergansers and smews. The red-breasted merganser's Latin name, *Mergus serrata*, refers to these impressive serrated bills, which the sawbills use to seize and hold fish before swallowing whole.

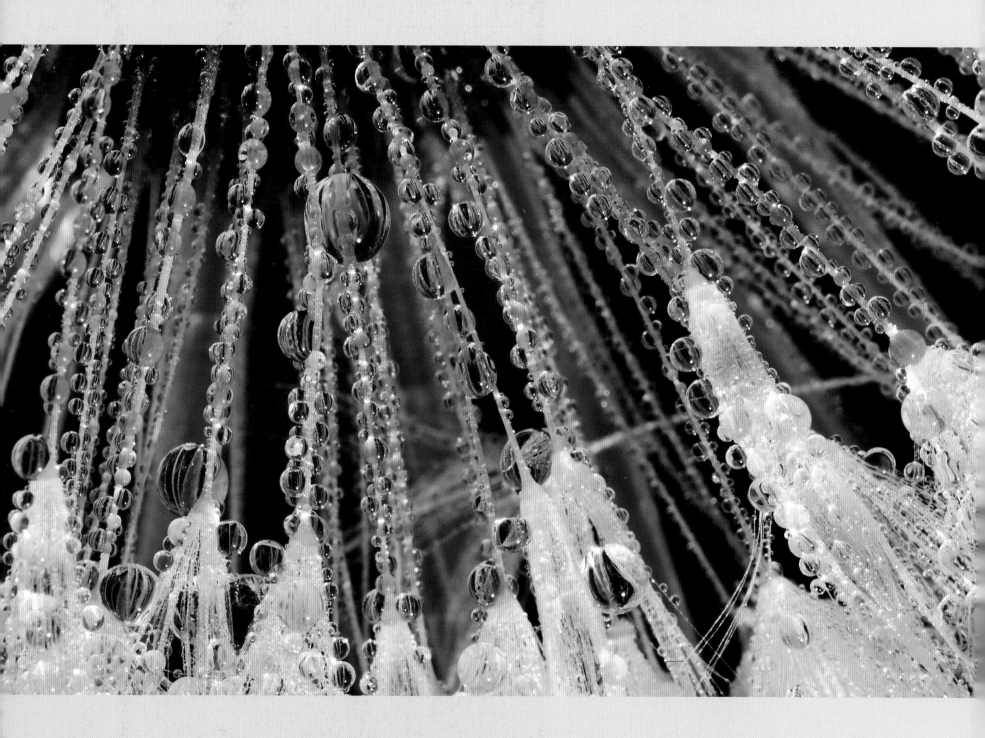

A Bigger Picture

Kevin the chameleon clasps my wrist with his two-pronged feet, his eyes rotating like mini turrets in their yellow-green rims. You couldn't dream up a science-fiction creature weirder than this. Kevin shares the Campbell family's bright living room, dwelling in a spacious tank beside an awesome collection of natural history and photography books from around the world. Tom the corn snake lives in the opposite corner, and two geckos share a tank beside the door.

It all stems from Laurie's schooldays and summer evenings exploring the beaches south of Berwick-upon-Tweed. There he discovered exquisite little reptiles basking in the sunshine. He caught one and held it – it was like something from prehistory or storybooks, a miniature dragon or dinosaur right there in the palm of his hand. His natural history books later informed him they were viviparous lizards, also known as common lizards. He caught some to take home – and has been keeping reptiles ever since.

We take Kevin through to the kitchen; he likes to hang out on the umbrella plant, with a view to the world outside. Laurie feeds him locusts while we spread out notebooks, discuss otters in Ardnamurchan. Outside the light is fading. We need to head out if we want to reach the river before dark.

We meet up with Laurie's friend Derek on a bridge over the Tweed. Derek is both a geologist and conservation advisor with deep roots in the Borders; he knows the rivers and landscape and people and history of this area, and meeting him is like finding a rich seam of stories. He and Laurie have spent many evenings and early mornings on this bridge, comparing wildlife notes and watching otters on the river below.

There are no signs of otters here tonight, though, so we walk along the bank-side path for a while and settle on a bench beside the river. The trees around us are black silhouettes now, but the sky behind them is still bright. Derek tells us how the river is the focal point for everything around here, the area's most precious resource, its lifeblood.

We share otter stories. Derek's dad remembers the Dumfriesshire Otter Hounds working the river island in Kelso. He recalls speaking with the huntsmen in the early 1970s and hearing that they weren't catching many otters, and those that they did catch were sick. So it took about twenty years for the pollutants to work their way out of the system, and a further twenty years for the population to recover to its previous levels. That's my lifetime. Derek is refreshingly optimistic about how much has been, and can be, achieved in one generation. How the wild world can restore itself, given half a chance and a helping hand.

Derek's first otter sighting was of a wee face peeping out of a tangle of gorse and ash and soft rush and meadowsweet. He'd been watching a large gorse stand, as there were otter tracks in and out and all around it, 'like Piccadilly Circus for otters'. He reads the tracks in the morning to discover the stories of the night. At Roxburgh Castle one morning there were otter slides in the dewy grass all the way down the hundred-foot slope from the castle to the moat. Scientists frown at the suggestion that otters slide and play for the sheer hell of it, but it's hard to think why else they'd spend the night climbing up and sliding down the castle slope.

On the riverside bench we share silence too, a comfortable and companionable silence, just watching the darkening river. Swans come gliding by; the scruffy cygnets are barely discernible dark shapes, but the adults gleam white in the last of the light.

The next morning dawns soft and utterly still. I feel a tug of conscience as I pull on my wellies and pack my binoculars. It's time to get this book finished and we really should be working indoors now – sorting photos into folders, checking captions. But the light is sweet and enticing, and the lure of the river-bank is irresistible.

So we're up on the Union Chain Bridge that links Scotland and England, looking down on the morning mist, a magical, wispy swirl floating over the river and catching the early sun with a glare of white. I can't help smiling as we head down from the bridge and take the path along the misty river towards Paxton House. The bank-side trees are tinged with colour, just about to turn. Beside us blackberries are ripe and plump and shining in the morning light. I snatch them as we pass, suck their sweetness from my stained fingers.

Laurie carries two large tripods on his shoulder, a heavy bag of lenses as well as binoculars round his neck. The burden of it all is easier to bear than the frustration of a missed opportunity through not having an important piece of equipment to hand. I ask would he still get a kick out of just seeing something amazing, even if he couldn't photograph it? He winces at the thought, as if he's in pain.

Then Laurie stops, alert and silent, listening, hands reaching for his camera. There's a clear, high-pitched whistle. Laurie nods in the direction of the sound, alerting me to an elegant silhouette of a long-beaked bird on a rock at the water's edge.

'Kingfishers don't usually perch on rocks,' he whispers, smiling. But this one did, just for a moment. Then it lifts in the air and hovers, its silhouette blurred at the edges by its wing beats, its brilliant colours eclipsed against the celestial white of morning sun on mist. Then it loops across the river and away.

We wait and watch in silence for a while, but it doesn't return. Laurie takes close-ups of the beech leaves we're peering through.

'It's a bit like why ospreys build frustration nests when their original one fails,' he explains. 'I need to come back with something.' Over on the opposite bank, a black-headed gull on a rock looks lonesome and scruffy in its winter plumage, the fine chocolate-brown of its summer head reduced to a smudgy patch beside its eye. A sure indication that the year is moving on.

A bit further upstream we paddle into the still river to check for signs of otters on a secluded stretch of bank. We find otter prints at the water's edge. The thrill of their presence ripples through me. Gilded circles of light flow outwards from our wellies as we walk, and minnows skit across our shadows in the shallow water.

We walk on, heading homewards now. It's too late to be looking for otters themselves. But I realise, with a flicker of surprise, that I feel no disappointment. I'm smiling at the sweetness of the morning, the joy of being here today. I first came to this river longing for otters, searching, yearning to see them. Now something has changed and my focus broadened, my experience is richer and more textured. The presence of otters, whether seen or unseen, delights me no less, but somewhere along the way I've become enchanted with the whole of this place – the plants and the birds and the river itself, and the people I've met, and the way it all connects. I'm reaching for blackberries again when Laurie stops. He's staring into the grassy bank with intense concentration. I can't figure out what's stopped him in his tracks, and I don't want to ask in case I'm missing something obvious or I disturb whatever it is. There's nothing much there – just long grass and nettles and dying-down plants, like the scraggly, end-of-season dandelion seed heads without much seed left.

Laurie's silent, engrossed. I copy the silence and wait, scanning for clues. Then he starts setting up his tripod, changing lenses, talking about close-up work being all about the precision and placing of the camera, keeping it flush with the subject. It is the dandelions. He's peering down at one through his lens, scolding the breeze for moving it, though the day seems so still, and the sun for being too bright already. There's a sharp, rasping bark from the woods beyond the fields.

'Hear that roe deer?' Laurie asks, without moving, still peering through the lens.

Then Laurie shows me what he's seen. In the camera's screen the dandelion is rendered magnificent. Its remaining seeds form an opulent sculpture of silk and glass, jewelled with beads of dew, its beauty revealed because he has noticed it.